ON THE MUSICALLY BEAUTIFUL

EDUARD HANSLICK AT AGE 40
After the collograph frontispiece to the
first volume of his autobiography
Aus meinem Leben (1894)

EDUARD HANSLICK

ON THE MUSICALLY BEAUTIFUL:

A Contribution towards the Revision of the Aesthetics of Music

Translated and Edited by

GEOFFREY PAYZANT

from the Eighth Edition (1891) of

VOM MUSIKALISCH-SCHÖNEN:

ein Betrag zur Revision der Ästhetik der Tonkunst

HACKETT PUBLISHING COMPANY

Printed in the United States of America

10 9 8 7 6 5 4 3 2   90 91 92 93 94 95 96 97 98 99

For further information, please address

    Hackett Publishing Company
    Box 44937
    Indianapolis, Indiana 46204

Cover design by Listenberger Design Associates
Interior design by Dan Kirklin

Library of Congress Cataloging in Publication Data

Hanslick, Eduard, 1825-1904.
  [Vom Musikalisch-Schönen. English]
  On the musically beautiful.

  Translation of: Vom Musikalisch-Schönen.
  English translation from the 8th ed. (1891).
  Bibliography: p.
  Includes index.
  1. Music – Philosophy and aesthetics.   I. Payzant,
Geoffrey, 1926–   II. Title.
ML3847.H3   1986   780'.1   85-27249
ISBN 0-87220-015-9
ISBN 0-87220-014-0 (pbk.)

Ten German editions of *Vom Musikalisch-Schönen* appeared in Eduard Hanslick's lifetime; five of them, including the Eighth Edition here translated, are dedicated to Robert Zimmermann. The translation is dedicated to Clemens Höslinger.

CONTENTS

ACKNOWLEDGMENTS

To paraphrase Hanslick in his foreword, I am very keenly aware of the short-comings of this translation. For these I alone am to blame, and none of the people who have assisted in various ways, including: Theophil Antonicek, Arnold Berleant, Steven Burns, Rainer Bischof, Eva Cooper, Hans Eichner, Gordon Epperson, Kurt Rudolf Fischer, Andrea Held, Clemens Höslinger, Oleh Hornykiewicz, Janet Kirkconnell, Peter Kivy, Hans-Dieter Klein, Hans Leitner, Maria Rika Maniates, Robert McRae, Otto Rauchbauer, Wolfgang Siegel, and Francis Sparshott. I am exceedingly grateful to them.

I thank also the Humanities and Social Sciences Committee of the Research Board of the University of Toronto for the award of grants in aid of my researches in Vienna in 1981–82, 1983, and 1985 in connection with the preparation of this translation.

TRANSLATOR'S PREFACE

Eduard Hanslick is the most successful and influential aesthetician of music of our time. His famous *Vom Musikalisch-Schönen* was first published in 1854, and in 1897 was in its ninth edition. It has had widespread influence among both specialists and laymen. Opinion is more or less evenly divided between those who are in agreement with it and those who are in disagreement. The book has survived all challenges, and today it is read as much, and with as much enjoyment, as it was forty years ago.[1]

So wrote Paul Moos in his *Moderne Musikästhetik in Deutschland* (1902). In 1922 Moos said the same in the second edition of his book, except that he reported the publication of the twelfth edition of *Vom Musikalisch-Schönen* in 1918.[2] 1922 was the year of the so-called "13th to 15th"[3] edition of Hanslick's book; this is still in print.[4] In that year Rudolf Schäfke, another historian of musical aesthetics, in his *Eduard Hanslick und die Musikästhetik,* quoted from recent contributions to the debate over the book and wrote: "Obviously the Hanslick problem has not yet gone away."[5]

Nor has it in the years since. Concerning *Vom Musikalisch-Schönen,* these words of Morris Weitz appeared in 1957: "[It] has become a classic in musical aesthetics and, in my opinion, remains the best introduction to the subject. It is to music what Hume's *Inquiry Concerning Human Understanding* is to speculative philosophy, a devastating critique of unsupportable views and an attempt to state clearly and precisely the territories and boundaries of the areas they discuss.[6]

Nobody who is familiar with the literature on musical aesthetics could seriously disagree with these assessments of Hanslick's book and of its influence, but there is a remarkable disproportion between its influence and the author's modest intentions in writing it.

In August 1854 Eduard Hanslick was not yet aged thirty; he had a doctorate in law from the University of Vienna, and was an official in the government service. The following announcement appeared in a Viennese literary journal (all translations in this volume are mine, except where otherwise noted):

> Dr. Eduard Hanslick, who is one of the most highly regarded contributors to these pages, has achieved an enviable reputation in the sphere of musical criticism. A small book by him will appear very soon from the publisher R. Weigel in Leipzig under the title "Towards a Revision of the Aesthetics of Music" ["Zur Revision der Aesthetik der Tonkunst"]. From a thorough-going and serious study of the philosophical-aesthetical literature, Dr. Hanslick has arrived at a theoretical perspective which he combines with a considerable experience of practical music-making. The work critically examines the fundamental principles of music and vigorously opposes traditional prejudices, so we may expect that it will capture the attention, not only of music-lovers, but of all who might favour a brilliant theoretical account of music, an art which on its empirical side appears to be so unproblematical.[7]

Presumably the announcement was written by Hanslick himself or by the journal's editor, Rudolf von Eitelberger, who had already published a long excerpt from the book in four instalments. It was through Eitelberger's good offices that it found a publisher in Leipzig, after having been refused by the two most important publishing houses in Vienna.[8]

Hanslick's book came out a month or so following this announcement, but under a very different title: *On the Musically Beautiful* (*Vom Musikalisch-Schönen*), with a slightly augmented version of its previously announced title as its subtitle: *A Contribution towards the Revision of the Aesthetics of Music* (*Ein Beitrag zur Revision der Ästhetik der Tonkunst*).[9]

The earlier title more accurately reflects the subject matter of the book, but there is no denying that both versions of the title are ugly and uninviting. Apparently someone, perhaps the publisher Rudolf Weigel (or Weigl) in Leipzig, took the view that this might have an adverse effect upon sales of the book, hence the more pretentious but catchy title "On the Musically Beautiful." However, the trouble with this title is that it strongly suggests that the book is something its author rightly insists it is not, namely a full-scale aesthetics of music. I translate here the whole of Hanslick's Foreword to the first edition of *On the Musically Beautiful*:

> Scarcely anyone who is familiar with it will deny that musical aesthetics as we know it stands in need of a thorough revision.
> It is the purpose of this book to set forth in full the principles to which such a revision must adhere in its critical and constructive function.
> The presumption is well-nigh epidemic among writers of monographs on musical aesthetics that a complete aesthetics of music lies dormant in their pages. I am a long way from making this presumption. Only in a restricted sense do I consider a complete musical aesthetics to be a possibility. To produce one, even in that sense, is beyond my present intentions and capabilities.

It will suffice if I succeed in bringing triumphant battering-rams against the decaying walls of the "feeling-theory" and in setting out a few cornerstones for future reconstruction. I am all too aware of the deficiencies in my account and reconcile myself with the thought that in due course I will have the opportunity to treat in greater detail the basic principles expounded here. If the present attempt manages to contribute towards bringing musical pleasure and appreciation closer to their only true foundation, namely the aesthetical, then it will have compensated me fully for the considerable amount of disfavour it is likely to bring me.[10]

The subsequent history of musical aesthetics might have been very different if the title under which this book appeared had not given Hanslick's adversaries so irresistible an opportunity to attack it as something much more ambitious than it actually was.

What must we do if we are to make a new beginning in musical aesthetics? We must first clear away the rubble of obsolete prejudices and presuppositions, then mark out the foundations upon which a new theory might be built. These alone are Hanslick's avowed and manifest purposes in writing the book. He does not claim to be building the new theory, although he reserves the right eventually to attempt such an undertaking. But for reasons he gave forty years later in his autobiography, he never got around to doing this:

Of course it was my intention, when I had time, to expand my essay *On the Musically Beautiful* into a proper aesthetics of music. It was as obvious to me that the essay was only a kind of preliminary sketch or ground plan as it was that its negative, polemical part was too long and too harsh compared to the positive, systematic part. But a full-scale and systematic aesthetics of music would be an undertaking demanding sustained effort and undivided attention. In those early years that was out of the question. Anyone for whom the first and better part of the day is taken up by the demands of the government service can perhaps in the rest of it carry on the profession of music critic (certainly not an undemanding one in Vienna) and write articles for journals, but not a systematic work in philosophy. So when I exchanged my position as a government official for that of an associate professor [at the University of Vienna] in the autumn of 1861, I acquired more free time for my studies, but they had been gradually changing direction.
Over several years I had studied so many "Aesthetics" of this and that, so many treatises on the nature of music, and had read so much in connection with my own book, that I was oversaturated with philosophizing about music and was tired of wrestling with abstract concepts. By contrast I found escape and endless pleasure in the history of music. From this study I came to the conviction that a truly fruitful aesthetics of music would have to be either based upon a profound historical awareness or developed hand-in-hand with it. What is the musically beautiful? Obviously different times, different peoples, and different schools have answered the question in altogether different ways. The further I went into the history of music, the more I found abstract musical aesthetics shimmering before my eyes, like a mirage. It seemed to me that a work deserving the title "Aesthetics of Music" was still a long way from being feasible.[11]

In this quotation, the word I have translated as "ground plan" is *Grundbau,* of which "foundation" would be a more literal rendering. A synonym of *Grundbau* is *Grundlage,* which brings to mind Immanuel Kant's *Grundlegung zur Metaphysik der Sitten,* a translation of which is available in the present series under the title *Grounding for the Metaphysics of Morals.*[12] Hanslick's *Vom Musikalisch-Schönen* is related to his unwritten aesthetics of music as is Kant's *Grundlegung* to his *Die Metaphysik der Sitten* or his *Kritik der Praktischen Vernunft.* In the *Grundlegung* Kant says that he regards the study of the foundations of a science (e.g., the science of morals) as separable from the study of that science itself. Hanslick, like Kant, clearly states that his work is merely a foundation; *Vom Musikalisch-Schönen* is no more an aesthetics of music than is Kant's *Grundlegung* an ethics. Yet in each case there has been no lack of commentators who insist on regarding the foundation as a failed attempt to construct an edifice.

Just to complete this fleeting comparison of Hanslick with Kant, we should note that for Kant the foundation of the science of morals is a principle or law, the so-called "categorical imperative," which we need not try to characterize here. For Hanslick the foundation of the science of musical aesthetics is an account of the essence of musical artworks, regarded objectively and not from the point of view of our physical and emotional responses to them.

Eduard Hanslick's philosophical career began and ended with the producing of this little book; he did not participate directly in the lively debate it provoked. This is not to say that he was philosophically inept or naive; no careful reading of his book will yield that impression. But, as is apparent from his remarks just quoted and from his Foreword to the edition here translated, his interest in writing it was more polemical than philosophical, although it is because of its philosophical significance that it has survived and become a classic. Throughout his career Hanslick was engaged in cultural politics, particularly with regard to music and theatre, beginning with his first appearance in print. This was in December 1844, in a Prague journal named *Ost und West;* Hanslick was then only nineteen.[13] Ostensibly a review of a performance of Gluck's *Armida,* his article was actually a vigorous attack on the local opera management for what Hanslick considered its excessively conservative programming. Half a century later, the indignation still fresh in his memory, Hanslick complained in his autobiography that his comparison of Gluck's admirers in Prague with the early Christians in the catacombs was deleted by "the censor." Moderation in expression seldom came readily to Hanslick when matters of musical principle were involved – at any rate, not until years after he wrote *Vom Musikalisch-Schönen.*

Eduard Hanslick had the benefit of a quite exceptional philosophical upbringing. From childhood until Gymnasium, his teacher of philosophy (and of almost everything else) was his father, Josef Adolf Hanslik (1785-1859).[14] In his youth J. A. Hanslik aspired to the priesthood and duly entered a seminary. There, along with theology, he no doubt studied the official "school" philosophy, based upon Aristotle and Aquinas. He had a crisis of faith and gave up his religious vocation, but philosophy, especially aesthetics, remained his chief intellectual preoccupation for the rest of his life. For a time he held a position teaching aesthetics at the Hochschule in Prague. He edited for posthumous publication a manuscript on aesthetics by a colleague; it was in Kantian vein.[15] He was also an accomplished pianist and a singer.

Family circumstances enabled J. A. Hanslik to devote much of his time to the instruction of his offspring, greatly to their advantage, according to Eduard's recollections. He continued participating in Eduard's philosophical development through Gymnasium and the two "philosophical years" (actually more theological than philosophical) at the University of Prague, reading his son's written assignments and preparing for him abstracts of various philosophical texts. The writings of the philosopher Friedrich Eduard Beneke (1798-1854) were a special interest of J. A. Hanslik's; he owned copies of all Beneke's published works and cherished a portrait of him. Beneke based his philosophy upon an empiricistic psychology and was regarded as a "materialist," a label which was contemptuously but perhaps erroneously attached to Eduard Hanslick, following the publication of *Vom Musikalisch-Schönen* in 1854.

Another personal influence upon Eduard Hanslick's philosophical outlook was his close friend Robert Zimmermann, who, at the time Hanslick was writing *Vom Musikalisch-Schönen,* was well established in a distinguished career as a professor of philosophy. Hanslick dedicated several of the different editions of his book, including the one here translated, to Zimmermann; we are tempted to say that this was the least he could do to acknowledge his debt.[16]

Zimmermann, like F. E. Beneke, was a follower of Johann Friedrich Herbart (1776-1841), a major figure in nineteenth-century German philosophy and psychology. Some historians of aesthetics and some commentators on Hanslick's book consider it a work in Herbartian philosophy,[17] but this connection (like almost everything else that has been said of the book) has been questioned.[18]

From Beneke by way of J. A. Hanslik and from Herbart by way of Zimmermann comes Eduard Hanslick's conviction that an exact science of aesthetics was possible and would succeed rhapsodic treatments of the subject, such as those he attacks in his first two chapters. This conviction is more stridently expressed in the first than in the second and subsequent editions of *Vom Musikalisch-Schönen.*

If we wish to trace the philosophical influences upon Hanslick, we must from this point proceed with caution. As Carl Dahlhaus has remarked, Hanslick's position is tricky (*prekär*) so far as the history of ideas is concerned.[19]

Of course there are interesting comparisons to be made between specific passages in Hanslick and specific passages in the writings of Kant, but we have neither internal nor collateral evidence upon which to make a positive claim for an influence from the one to the other, except perhaps indirectly by way of C. F. Michaelis.[20] Schopenhauer is not mentioned in Hanslick's book by name; there are two apparent allusions to him, both trivial. Hegel is named, quoted, and alluded to, not on trivial matters, but there is no argument in Hanslick, no point of doctrine, to which we can confidently point and declare that it is of Hegelian origin.

Several likely candidates have been proposed in the literature for the distinction of being major influences upon Hanslick in the writing of this book; much work remains to be done in this area. I believe that insufficient attention has been given to Hanslick's earlier writings. In these we can see him working out the basic ideas of *Vom Musikalisch-Schönen,* stimulated not so much by philosophers as by two composers who were also prolific writers on music: Hector Berlioz and Alfred Julius Becher.[21]

Many authors philosophically more competent than Hanslick have written on musical aesthetics before and since, but few equally accomplished musicians. From his father, and later from Wenzel Tomaschek at the Prague Conservatory, he had a fully professional training in piano, composition, and the history and theory of music. Herein lies the special strength of *Vom Musikalisch-Schönen:* that from childhood its author was actively engaged in music and music-making and that from adolescence he was in a position to think aloud in print about music, in front of an audience of readers who took even his most extravagant pronouncements seriously, pro or contra.

A few words on the structure of Hanslick's book might be helpful. The first two chapters elaborate and defend his negative thesis that it is not the essential purpose of music to arouse, express, or portray human feelings. In these two chapters he produces his "triumphant battering-rams," namely seven or eight specific arguments against what he says is the prevailing theory in musical aesthetics, the "feeling-theory." He by no means claims that music *cannot* arouse, express, or portray feelings; obviously it can do all these things. He merely says that to do so is not the defining purpose of music.

Chapter 3 has essentially the same title as the book itself. It is the chapter most frequently included in volumes of readings in aesthetics, for the very good reason that it contains the basic account of Hanslick's positive doctrine of the musically beautiful, an account which is completed in the final chapter of the book, Chapter 7. Readers of the present translation are referred to the "Essay: Towards a Revised Reading of Hanslick" at the back of this volume for an introduction to the central ideas of Chapter 3.

Chapters 4 and 5 investigate the psychological and physiological conditions of musical awareness in its various aspects and set forth the important distinction between the "aesthetical" and the "pathological" responses to music. Of course the psychology and physiology in these two chapters are obsolete, but Hanslick's theorizing in connection with them is penetrating and original. That chapters 4 and 5 appeared in print about a year before the book was published suggests that Hanslick considered them of particular importance to an understanding of his theorizing, even an introduction to it.[22]

Chapter 6 is the (at that time) obligatory chapter on the relation of music to nature; it concludes that there is no such relation, at least so far as aesthetical theory is concerned. This chapter is especially valuable for its treatment of the concept of "material" in music.

Chapter 7, as noted above, completes the positive doctrine introduced in Chapter 3 and amplifies it in a few important respects. This chapter provides an ending but not a conclusion, which is in keeping with Hanslick's stated intention that the book should be nothing more than a beginning, an attempt to provide a new foundation for a scientific aesthetics of music.

Not, however, a foundation for a scientific aesthetics of all music. It will be remembered that in his Foreword to the first edition, quoted above, Hanslick speaks of the "restricted sense" in which he considers an aesthetics of music to be possible. He does not tell us what it is that imposes the restriction, but we have a clue to it in the above quotation from his autobiography. There he says that different times, different peoples, and different schools have different views on what constitutes the musically beautiful. Looking back on his long career as a writer on music, he says wryly that for him the history of music began with Bach and Handel but that in his heart it began with Mozart and reached its summit in Beethoven, Schumann, and Brahms.[23] It would seem that, for Hanslick, the fundamental principle of music, namely the musically beautiful, while objective (i.e., not determined by our responses to it), is not universal but is culturally and historically conditioned. His book, then, is more accurately described as an essay towards the revision of the aesthetics of music belonging to what we may call the Great Tradition, Mozart to Brahms.

My Preface has emphasized the limitations of *Vom Musikalisch-Schönen,* at least so far as its author has brought them to our attention. This is not to raise doubts concerning the book's importance. Far from it: To have set out a foundation for an aesthetics of European music from Mozart to Brahms is no small achievement. That Hanslick's proposals are still under lively philosophical debate is an indication that to some extent he succeeded.

Hanslick said that it seemed to him (in the 1890s) "that a work deserving the title 'Aesthetics of Music' was still a long way from being feasible." Perhaps it still is. When the time comes to attempt such a thing, however, if it is not built upon Hanslick's foundation, at the least it will have to be built around it.

G. P.

Toronto
April 9, 1986

BIBLIOGRAPHY

1. Three German reprints of Eduard Hanslick's *Vom Musikalisch-Schönen* are available: the First Edition of 1854 (Darmstadt: Wissenschaftliche Buchgesellschaft, 1981); the so-called Thirteenth to Fifteenth Edition of 1922 (Wiesbaden: Breitkopf und Härtel, successive years and printings); the same edition in a volume edited by Klaus Mehner, *Hanslick: Vom Musikalisch-Schönen; Aufsätze; Musikkritiken* (Leipzig: Reclam, 1982). The present translation is of the Eighth Edition of 1891, which is in all important respects similar to the second and third of these reprints.

2. Gustav Cohen translated the Seventh Edition (1885) of Hanslick's *Vom Musikalisch-Schönen* as *The Beautiful in Music* (London and New York: Novello, 1891). The original edition of this translation is available in reprint (New York: Da Capo, 1974).

3. Other writings by Hanslick (available in German): Many of Hanslick's essays, feuilletons, and critical writings were republished in collections under various titles from 1875 to 1900 (Berlin: Hoffmann, for the Allgemeine Verein für Deutsche Literatur); his autobiography *Aus meinem Leben* (two volumes, 1894) appeared under the same imprints. All these and his *Geschichte des Concertwesens in Wien* (originally two volumes published separately by Braumüller in Vienna 1869 and 1870) are available in reprint (1971) from Gregg International Publishers, Farnborough, Hants., England. The *Geschichte* is also available in reprint (1979) from Georg Olms Verlag, Hildesheim and New York.

4. Other writings by Hanslick (in English translation): A volume of musical criticisms by Hanslick, translated and edited by Henry Pleasants III, appeared in 1950 with the title *Vienna's Golden Years of Music, 1850-1900* (New York: Simon and Schuster). A reprint is available (Freeport, N.Y.: Books for Libraries, 1969). The volume contains an introductory essay on Hanslick by Henry Pleasants III.

5. Some writings in German about Hanslick's musical aesthetics: W. Abegg, *Musikästhetik und Musikkritik bei Eduard Hanslick*, Regensburg: Bosse, 1974; C. Dahlhaus, "Eduard Hanslick und der musikalische Formbegriff," *Die Musikforschung* 20 (1967), pp. 145-53; C. Dahlhaus, "Rhythmus im Großen," *Melos/NZ* 1 (1975),

pp. 439-41; D. Glatt, *Zur Geschichtlichen Bedeutung der Musikaesthetik Eduard Hanslicks,* Munich: Katzbichler, 1972; R. Schäfke, *Eduard Hanslick und die Musikästhetik,* Leipzig: Breitkopf & Härtel, 1922, reprint Nendeln/Lichtenstein: Kraus, 1976.

6. Some writings in English about Hanslick's musical aesthetics: M. Budd, "The Repudiation of Emotion: Hanslick on Music," *British Journal of Aesthetics* 20 (1980), pp. 29-43; S. Deas, *In Defence of Hanslick,* London: Williams and Norgate, 1940, reprint Farnborough, Hants., England: Gregg International, 1972; G. Epperson, *The Musical Symbol,* Ames: Iowa State University Press, 1967, pp. 107-25, reprint New York: Da Capo, 1986; R. Hall, "On Hanslick's Supposed Formalism in Music," *Journal of Aesthetics and Art Criticism* 25 (1967), pp. 434-36; J. Hospers, *Meaning and Truth in the Arts,* Chapel Hill: University of North Carolina Press, 1946, pp. 78-98; G. Payzant, "Hanslick, Sams, Gay, and 'tönend bewegte Formen'," *Journal of Aesthetics and Art Criticism* 40 (1981), pp. 41-48; G. Payzant, "Eduard Hanslick and the 'geistreich' Dr. Alfred Julius Becher," *The Music Review* 44 (1983), pp. 104-15; G. Payzant, "Eduard Hanslick on the Rôle of the Performer," in *Opuscula aesthetica nostra,* edited by C. Cloutier and C. Seerveld, Edmonton: Academic Printing and Publishing, 1984, pp. 73-80.

7. On Hanslick as critic: P. Gay, *Freud, Jews and Other Germans,* New York: Oxford University Press, 1978, ch. 6; E. Sams, "Eduard Hanslick, 1825-1904: the Perfect Wagnerite," *Musical Times* 116 (1975), pp. 867-68.

8. Two eyewitness accounts of Hanslick: M. Graf, *Composer and Critic: Two Hundred Years of Musical Criticism,* New York: Norton, 1946, pp. 244-51; R. Specht, *Johannes Brahms,* translated by E. Blom, London: J. M. Dent and Sons, 1930, pp. 170-75.

9. Myths, misconceptions, and calumnies about Hanslick exposed: C. Höslinger, "Einige Anmerkungen zum Thema Hanslick," *Österreichische Musikzeitschrift* 21 (1966), pp. 535-44.

FOREWORD TO THE EIGHTH EDITION

The first edition of this work appeared in 1854; nothing is new in the present edition, the eighth, except the more convenient format and more attractive layout. In text it differs from the seventh edition (1885) in only a few minor corrections. I would like to introduce this new edition with the words used by the admirable F. T. Vischer in the reprint of one of his earlier essays, "Der Traum":

> I include this essay in the present collection without defending it against the attacks it has received. And I have refrained from any but minor improvements. Perhaps nowadays I would have put some of it another way, would have taken more pains to explain, would have been more restrained. Who is ever entirely pleased with a work when he reads it many years after he wrote it? Yet everyone knows that by meddling with it we are as likely to make it worse as better.*

If I cared to engage here in polemics, replying to all the criticisms to which my little book has given rise, it would expand to an alarming thickness. My convictions remain unchanged, and so does the absolute opposition of certain contemporary musical factions. So the reader will perhaps permit me to repeat a few comments which I included in the third edition.

---

*"Altes und Neues" von Fr. Th. Vischer (Stuttgart 1881). S. 187.[1] [Many of Hanslick's quotations and citations are incomplete or incorrect in one way or another; as late as 1982, a completely reset German edition of *Vom Musikalisch-Schönen* appeared, with these defects carefully preserved. So far as the requirements of a translation permit, I have shown Hanslick's versions unaltered in the main text. My corrections of them are in the Translator's Notes, hence the many discrepancies between footnotes and their corresponding Notes. In the present instance, for example, Hanslick has the year of publication wrong. – *Translator.*]

I am very keenly aware of the shortcomings of this essay. Yet the favourable reception of earlier editions, which far exceeded expectations, and the immensely gratifying sympathy with which eminent specialists in both philosophy and music responded to it, convinced me that my ideas, even in the somewhat caustic and rhapsodic manner of their original appearance, fell on good soil. To my very happy surprise, I found a remarkable agreement with these ideas in Grillparzer's sketches and aphorisms concerning music, which appeared posthumously ten years ago; I could not forbear quoting a few of the most notable of these sayings in this new edition. They are treated more fully in my essay "Grillparzer und die Musik."*

Ardent opponents have accused me from time to time of mounting a full-scale polemic against everything that goes by the name of feeling, whereas every impartial and attentive reader can easily see that I protest only against the erroneous involvement of feeling in science and thus strive against those aesthetical visionaries who, while pretending to tell musicians what to do, merely expose their own tinkling opium dreams.

I share completely the view that the ultimate worth of the beautiful is always based on the immediate manifestness of feeling.[2] However, I hold just as firmly the conviction that, from all the customary appeals to feeling, we can derive not a single musical law.

This conviction constitutes the one main thesis, a negative one, of this inquiry. The thesis first and foremost opposes the widespread view that music is supposed to "represent feelings." It is incomprehensible to me the way some people insist that this implies an absolute lack of feeling in music. The rose is fragrant, but we do not say that its content is the representation of fragrance; the forest diffuses shady coolness, but it does not represent the feeling of shady coolness. It is not idle bickering to argue emphatically against the concept of "representation," since from this concept have arisen the most serious errors in the aesthetics of music. To "represent" something always involves the notion of two separate, dissimilar things, of which one must be intentionally related to the other through a particular mental act.

With a felicitous image, Emanuel Geibel has expressed this relationship, in couplets, more astutely and elegantly than philosophical analysis could:

---

*"Musikalische Stationen" von Ed. Hanslick. Berlin, Verein f. dt. Litt. 1885. 5. Aufl.[3]

Warum glückt es dir nie, Musik mit Worten zu schildern?
Weil sie, ein rein Element, Bild und Gedanken verschmäht.
Selbst das Gefühl ist nur wie ein sanft durchscheinender Flußgrund,
Drauf ihr klingender Strom schwellend und sinkend entrollt.*

If this beautiful epigram, moreover, resulted from the poet's impressions of my book, as I have reason to suppose it did, then my point of view, though for the most part disparaged by poetically minded people, is nevertheless not too incompatible with true poetry.

To the aforementioned thesis there is an antithesis: that the beauty of a piece of music is specifically musical, i.e., is inherent in the tonal relationships without reference to an extraneous, extramusical context. It was the sincere intention of the author to elucidate fully the "musically beautiful" as the vital issue of our art and the supreme principle of its aesthetics. If, however, the polemical and negative element took on an overemphasis in the realization of this intention, I hope the reader will pardon this, considering the special circumstances of the time. As I was writing this essay, the spokesmen for the "music of the future" were at their most vocal, inevitably provoking a reaction from people with convictions such as mine. And while I was working on the second edition, along came Liszt's so-called "program symphonies," which succeeded more completely than anything heretofore in getting rid of the autonomous significance of music and in suggesting to the listener that it is nothing but a means for the generation of musical configurations. Since then we have acquired also Richard Wagner's *Tristan* and *The Ring of the Nibelungen,* along with his doctrine of endless melody, i.e., formlessness raised to the level of a principle, and the sung and fiddled opium-trance for whose cult, if you please, a temple all its own has been dedicated in Bayreuth.

Perhaps it will count in my favour that, when faced with such portents, I felt no inclination to shorten or tone down the polemical side of my book, but on the contrary pointed even more urgently to the unique and imperishable in

---

Neue Gedichte.[4]

[Why does it never work out when you try to describe music in words?
Because it, a pure element, disdains images and thoughts.
Feeling, itself, is merely a smooth, visible riverbed
Upon which the resounding stream of feeling, swelling and subsiding, rolls away.

– *Translator.*]

music, i.e., musical beauty, and to how our great masters embodied it, and also to how genuine musical innovators will be cherished for all time.

ED. H.

Meran
September 11, 1891

I

THE AESTHETICS OF FEELING

Musical aesthetics up to now has for the most part laboured under a serious methodological error, in that it occupies itself, not so much with careful investigation of that which is beautiful in music, but rather with giving an account of the feelings which take possession of us when we hear it. The latter procedure is wholly consistent with those older systems of aesthetics which consider the beautiful only with regard to the sensations which it evokes in us and also, as is well known, consider that the philosophy of beauty has its origins in sensation ($αἴσθησις$).

In themselves unphilosophical, such systems in their application to the most ethereal of the arts degenerate somewhat into a kind of subjectivity, to the delight of dilettanti. But for the serious inquirer, they provide the least possible illumination. Whoever wants to learn about the objective nature of music wants to get out from under the dubious authority of feeling and not (as with most textbooks) be all the time harking back to feeling.

The striving for as objective as possible a scientific knowledge of things, of which the effects are being felt in all areas of knowledge in our time, must necessarily also have an impact upon the investigation of beauty. This investigation can proceed satisfactorily only by breaking away from a method which takes subjective feeling as its starting point and then returns to it after going on a poetical excursion around the outskirts of the topic. If it is not to be wholly illusory, this investigation will have to approach the method of the natural sciences, at least to the point of attempting to get alongside the thing itself[1] and seeking whatever among our thousandfold flickering impressions and feelings may be enduring and objective.

The aesthetics of poetry and of the visual arts are far in advance of that of music and have for the most part abandoned the delusion that the

1

aesthetics of any particular art may be derived through mere conformity to the general, metaphysical concept of beauty (of which, however, each of the arts has its own set of variants). The servile dependence of the various special aesthetics upon a supreme metaphysical principle of a general aesthetics is steadily yielding ground to the conviction that each particular art demands to be understood only of itself, through a knowledge of its unique technical characteristics. System-building is giving way to research firmly based on the axiom that the laws of beauty proper to each particular art are inseparable from the distinctive characteristics of its material and its technique.* The aesthetics of literature and that of the visual arts are going about the practical side of their business, namely criticism, already adhering to the principle that the primary object of aesthetical investigation is the beautiful object, not the feelings of the subject.

Music alone among the arts still seems incapable of achieving this objective standpoint. It firmly separates its theoretical/grammatical rules from its aesthetical investigations and prefers to keep them that way, the former as drily intellectual and the latter as lyrically sentimental as possible. Previous musical aesthetics has not been able to make the effort to confront squarely its subject matter, the musically beautiful, as an autonomous species of beauty. Instead, "feelings" keep coming back like an old spectre to haunt us in broad daylight. The musically beautiful is considered, now as previously, only on the side of its subjective impression. In books, newspaper criticisms, and in conversations, it is daily proclaimed that feelings constitute the sole aesthetical foundation of

---

*Robert Schumann has done much mischief with his statement: "the aesthetics of one art is that of all the others; only the material is different." (I, 43 der Gesammelten Schriften.)[2]

Grillparzer took a totally different view, and hit the mark with the following:

> The greatest disservice anyone could have rendered all the arts in Germany was to have lumped them all together in the name of "Art." Despite their having so many points of contact among them, the arts differ endlessly in their media and in the basic conditions of their practice. Whoever wishes to make a sharp basic distinction between music and poetic art must consider the effect of music upon sensation. It begins with activation of the nervous system and, after having aroused the feelings, ultimately makes its appeal to the intellect. Poetic art, however, begins by arousing our intellectual awareness and only through this acts upon our feelings; poetry participates initially in the sensuous only in rare cases. Music and poetic art thus follow directly opposed routes, the one intellectualizing the corporeal and the other corporealizing the intellectual.

(IX, 142 der sämtl. Werke.)[3]

music and that feelings alone are entitled to impose the limits of critical judgment.

According to this doctrine, music cannot entertain the intellect by means of concepts the way literature does, any more than it can the eye, as do the visual arts. Hence music must have as its vocation to act upon the feelings. "Music has to do with the feelings," we are told. This expression "has to do" is a characteristically vague utterance of previous musical aesthetics. In what the connection between music and the feelings (specific feelings connected with specific pieces of music) might consist, according to what natural laws music might work, and according to what laws of art it may be shaped – about all this the very people who "have to do" with it leave us entirely in the dark. However, when we allow our eyes to adjust a little, we arrive at the discovery that in the prevailing view of music the feelings play a double rôle.

Of music in the first of these two rôles, it is claimed that to arouse the delicate feelings is the defining purpose of music. In the second, the feelings are designated as the content of music, that which musical art presents in its works.

The two are similar in that both are false.

The first appears in the introduction to most textbooks on music; it can be briefly refuted. Beauty has no purpose at all. For it is mere form, which, of course, according to its content, can be applied to the most diverse purposes, without having any purpose of its own beyond itself. From the contemplation of beauty there may arise pleasant feelings in the contemplator, but these have nothing to do with beauty as such. I might very well show something beautiful to an observer for the specific purpose of giving him pleasure. But this purpose in itself would not be what made the thing beautiful. Beauty is and remains beauty even if no feelings are aroused and even if it be neither perceived nor thought.[4]

So of a purpose in this sense, concerning music as well, nothing can be said. The fact that this art is intimately related to our feelings in no way supports the view that the aesthetical significance of music resides in this relationship.

In order to examine the relationship more closely, we must rigorously distinguish between the concepts of feeling and sensation. In ordinary speech we accept that the two are interchangeable.

Sensation is the perception of a specific sense quality: this particular tone, that particular colour. Feeling is becoming aware of our mental state with regard to its furtherance or inhibition, thus of well-being or distress. If I simply perceive with my senses the odour, flavour, shape, colour, or tone of a thing, then I am being sensitive to those qualities. If melancholy, hope, happiness, or hatred noticeably elevate or depress my mental state, then I am feeling.* Beauty encounters first of all our sensation. But this is not the private preserve of beauty: beauty shares it with every kind of phenomenon. Sensation is the beginning and the prerequisite of aesthetical pleasure, and it constitutes initially the basis of feeling; feeling always presupposes a relation (often a complex relation) between itself and sensation. It takes no skill to stimulate sensation; a single tone, a single colour can do it. As we have already noticed, *feeling* and *sensation* have been used interchangeably. For the most part, however, the older aesthetical works have called *sensation* what we call *feeling.* Thus the earlier writers have been of the opinion that music should arouse our feelings and fill us with piety, love, rejoicing, and woe.

In fact, however, to induce these feelings in us is not the task of music or of any other art. Art first of all puts something beautiful before us. It is not by means of feeling that we become aware of beauty,† but by means of the imagination as the activity of pure contemplation.

It is remarkable how musicians and the older aestheticians concern themselves only with the contrast between feeling and understanding, as if the main thing did not lie directly between the two. Out of the imagination of the composer, the piece of music arises for the imagination of the listener. Certainly with regard to beauty, imagining is not mere contemplating, but contemplating with active understanding, i.e., conceiving and judging. Of course these processes occur so swiftly that we are unaware of them and are deceived into thinking that what, in truth, depends on several intermediate processes occurs immediately. The word *contemplation*[6] has long since been extended to include all sense appearances and not merely the visual. And it serves very well for what we do when we listen attentively to the sequence of tonal forms that is music. Imagination, moreover, is by no means an isolated domain; it draws its vital impulse from our sensation and rapidly transmits our sensations to intellect and feeling. But, for the real comprehension of beauty, these are peripheral considerations.

In pure contemplation the hearer takes in nothing but the piece of music

---

*In this terminology the older philosophers tend to agree with the newer physiologists; certainly we must prefer it to that of the Hegelians, which, as is well known, distinguishes instead between inner and outer sensation.

†Hegel has pointed out that the investigation of the *sensation* (in our terminology, *feeling*) which an art produces leaves sensation wholly indeterminate and concentrates directly upon the proper concrete content of that art. He says: "what is felt remains enveloped in the form of the most abstract individual subjectivity, and therefore differences between feelings are also completely abstract, not differences in the thing itself" (Ästhetik I, 42).[5]

being played; every material interest must be set aside. The tendency to allow the feelings to become aroused is an interest of that sort. Exclusive preoccupation of mind through beauty operates logically instead of aesthetically; a predominant effect[7] upon feeling would be more questionable, would indeed be pathological.

All of this, derived long since from general aesthetics, is equally valid for the beauty that is in each of the arts. Thus, if we are to treat music as an art, we must recognize that imagination and not feeling is always the aesthetical authority. It seems advisable to state this modest premise because, considering the heavy emphasis unremittingly placed upon music's capacity for mitigating the human passions, we are sometimes not sure whether a piece of music is supposed to be a police order, a teaching aid, or a medical prescription.

Musicians, however, are less caught up in the mistake of wanting all the arts equally to lay claim upon the feelings; rather they see in this something specific to music. According to them, the power and inclination to arouse any feelings one pleases in the listener is precisely what distinguishes music from the other arts.*

The purpose of arousing such feelings in the listener, however, is no more the specific essence of music than it is the purpose of the arts as a whole. Once we grasp that the active imagination is the real organ of the beautiful, feeling will be admitted to be a secondary effect in each of the arts. Does a great historical painting not move us with the force of real life? Do Raphael's Madonnas not dispose us to devotion, Poussin's landscapes to wanderlust? Could we view Strasbourg Cathedral with no effects upon our feeling? The answer is not in doubt. And it applies also to poetry and indeed to many nonaesthetical preoccupations, such as religious fervor, rhetoric, etc. Thus we see that all the other arts likewise have strong effects upon feeling. We therefore must base the supposed essential difference between music and the other arts upon the relative strength of those effects. This solution is altogether unscientific, however, and moreover it rightly concedes to each person the decision whether he is more powerfully and profoundly moved by a Mozart symphony or a play of Shakespeare, by a poem of Uhland or by a Hummel rondo. If, however, we adopt the view that music works immediately upon feeling and the other arts work initially through the mediation of ideas, then this is the same error, but in different words, because, as we noticed, in the musically beautiful, feeling is nothing more than a secondary effect; only the

---

*Without separating *feeling* from *sensation,* we cannot investigate the varieties of the former: sensuous and intellectual feelings, with their chronic manifestation in temperament and their acute manifestations in affect, preference, and passion, as well as the peculiar shades of these in the Greek sense of *pathos* (Latin *passion*); all are indiscriminately flung together, and music is declared to be the art that arouses feeling.

imagination is immediately effective. In numerous treatises on music, the analogy is made between music and architecture; undoubtedly the analogy is a valid one. But has there ever been an architect in his right mind who took the view that architecture has the purpose of arousing feelings or that it has the feelings as its content?

Every genuine artwork stands in some kind of relation to our feeling, but none in an exclusive relation. Thus we say nothing at all concerning the crucial aesthetical principle of music if we merely characterize music in general, according to its effect upon feeling, just as little, perhaps, as we would get to know the real nature of wine by getting drunk. It depends solely upon the particular manner in which such feelings have been aroused by music. Thus, instead of clinging to secondary and vague feeling-effects of musical phenomena, we would do better to penetrate to the inner nature of the works and try, from the principles of their own structure, to account for the unique efficacy of the impressions we receive from them. Hardly any painter or poet persuades himself that he accounts for the beauty of his art when he inquires into the particular feeling his landscape or drama arouses. Instead, he traces the compelling power by which his work pleases and seeks to know why it pleases in just this way and no other. That this investigation (as we shall see later) is much more difficult in music than in the other arts, indeed that investigations of music can go only so far without getting out of hand, until recently entitled critics to confound the activation of feeling with the beauty in music instead of proceeding scientifically and representing the two as separately as possible.

Given that feeling can in no way be a basis for aesthetical principles, it is vitally important to be on guard against this firmly entrenched view concerning music and feeling. We mean here not the conventional prejudice made possible by the fact that our feelings and our mental images are frequently misled by verbal texts, titles, and other merely incidental associations of ideas (especially in church, military, and theatre music), which we are wrongly inclined to ascribe to the music itself. Rather, the connection between a piece of music and our changes of feeling is not at all one of strict causation; the piece changes our mood according to our changing musical experiences and impressions. Nowadays we can scarcely understand how our grandparents could regard some particular musical sequence as a precisely corresponding impression of a particular state of feeling. Evidence for this is the extraordinary difference between the reactions of Mozart's, Beethoven's, and Weber's contemporaries to their compositions and our own reaction today. How many works by Mozart were declared in his time to be the most passionate, ardent, and audacious within the reach of musical mood-painting. At that time, people contrasted the tranquillity and wholesomeness of Haydn's symphonies with the outbursts of vehement passion, bitter struggle, and piercing agony of

Mozart's.* Twenty or thirty years later, they made exactly the same comparison between Mozart and Beethoven. Mozart's position as representative of violent, inspired passion was taken over by Beethoven, and Mozart was promoted to Haydn's Olympian classicism. Any attentive musician who lives long enough will encounter similar metamorphoses. Nevertheless, throughout this variation in the impression of feeling, the musical value of many works remains in itself for us unaltered, their originality and beauty remaining as fresh as ever despite the excitement they might at one time have caused. Thus the connection between musical works and specific feelings does not apply always, in every case and necessarily, as an absolute imperative. This connection is incomparably more variable with regard to music than it is in any other art.

Thus the effect of music upon feeling possesses neither the necessity nor the exclusiveness nor the constancy which a phenomenon would have to exhibit in order to be the basis of an aesthetical principle.

The intense feelings which music awakens in us and all the moods, painful as well as delightful, into which it lulls us while we daydream: these we by no means wish to minimize. Indeed, it belongs to the most beautiful and redeeming mysteries that, by the grace of God, art is able to call forth such otherworldly stirrings in us. It is only against unscientific exploitation of these facts as aesthetical principles that we lodge our complaint. Joy and sorrow can in the highest degree be called into life by music; to this we entirely agree. But could not even more intense feeling be caused by winning a big prize in a lottery or by the mortal illness of a friend? So long as we are reluctant to include lottery tickets among the symphonies or medical reports among the overtures, we must not treat the feeling it in fact produces as an aesthetical specialty of music or of a particular composition. How such feelings will be aroused by music depends entirely upon the circumstances of each particular instance.

In Chapter IV and V we shall give very careful consideration to the influence of music upon feeling and investigate the positive side of this remarkable relationship. Here, at the beginning, in protest against an unscientific principle, its negative side could not be too vigorously swept away.†

---

*Particularly from Rochlitz come many such (to us) astonishing quotations regarding Mozart's instrumental music. He characterizes the charming Menuetto capriccio in Weber's Sonata in A-flat major as the "uninterrupted outpouring of a passionate, vehemently agitated spirit, yet held together with admirable firmness."8

†[See Appendix A: "Herbart" and Appendix B: "Some Feeling-Theorists."]

II

THE REPRESENTATION
OF FEELING IS NOT
THE CONTENT OF MUSIC

Partly as a consequence of this theory which pronounces the feelings to be the ultimate goal of musical effects and partly as a corrective to it, the proposition was formulated: Feelings are the content which music represents.

The philosophical investigation of an art raises the question of that art's content. Among the arts there is great diversity of content; related to this are fundamental differences in the way the various arts shape their products. These necessarily follow from differences among our senses, to which the arts are bound. Every art has as its own a range of ideas which it represents in its own medium of expression, e.g., tones, words, colours, stone. Accordingly, the particular artwork embodies a definite idea as beauty in sensuous appearance. This definite idea, its embodied form, and the unity of the two are conditions of the concept of beauty from which scientific investigation of an art can no longer be kept separate.

Whatever the content of a work of literary or visual art may be can be expressed in words and traced back to a concept: We say that this picture represents a flower girl, this statue a gladiator, that poem one of Roland's exploits.[1] The more or less perfect fusion of such a definite content into the artistic phenomenon, then, is the basis of our judgment concerning the beauty of the artwork.

There has been considerable agreement that the whole gamut of human feelings is the content of music, because feelings were considered to be the opposite of conceptual definiteness, hence they are a proper criterion for the distinction between music on the one hand and the visual and literary arts on the other. In this view, tones and their elaborate combination would be nothing more than raw material, the medium of expression, by means of which the composer represents love, courage, piety, rapture. These feelings, in their rich variety, would be the Idea which has attired itself in the earthly body of physical sound in order that it may walk on earth here below as a musical

8

artwork. That which in a lovely melody or an ingenious harmony delights and lifts us up would be not these in themselves but what they signify: the whisperings of amorousness, the violence of conflict.

In order to get on firm ground, we must first relentlessly get rid of such tired clichés. Whispering? Yes, but not the yearning of love. Violence? Of course, but certainly not the conflict. Music can, in fact, whisper, rage, and rustle. But love and anger occur only within our hearts.

The representation of a specific feeling or emotional state is not at all among the characteristic powers of music.

That is to say, the feelings are not so isolated in the mind that they have made themselves the salient feature of an art to which the representation of the other mental activities is closed. They are, on the contrary, dependent upon physiological and pathological conditions. They depend upon ideas, judgments, and (in brief) the whole range of intelligible and rational thought, to which some people so readily oppose feeling.

What, then, makes a feeling specific, e.g., longing, hope, love? Is it perhaps the mere strength or weakness, the fluctuations of our inner activity? Certainly not. These can be similar with different feelings, and with the same feeling they can differ from person to person and from time to time. Only on the basis of a number of ideas and judgments (perhaps unconsciously at moments of strong feeling) can our state of mind congeal into this or that specific feeling. The feeling of hope cannot be separated from the representation of a future happy state which we compare with the present; melancholy compares past happiness with the present. These are entirely specific representations or concepts. Without them, without this cognitive apparatus, we cannot call the actual feeling "hope" or "melancholy"; it produces them for this purpose. If we take this away, all that remains is an unspecific stirring, perhaps the awareness of a general state of well-being or distress. Love cannot be thought without the representation of a beloved person, without desire and striving after felicity, glorification and possession of a particular object. Not some kind of mere mental agitation, but its conceptual core, its real, historical content, specifies this feeling of love. Accordingly, its dynamic can appear as readily gentle as stormy, as readily joyful as sorrowful, and yet still be love. This consideration by itself suffices to show that music can only express the various accompanying adjectives and never the substantive, e.g., love itself. A specific feeling (a passion, say, or an affect) never exists as such without an actual historical content, which can only be precisely set forth in concepts. Music cannot (as if by way of compromise) render concepts as "indefinite speech." Is the result of all this not psychologically irrefutable? It is that music is incapable of expressing definite feelings; indeed, the definiteness of feelings lies precisely in their conceptual essence.

How it happens that music can nevertheless excite such feelings as melancholy, gaiety, and the like (can, not must) we shall investigate later, when we discuss the subjective impressions made by music. At present we shall merely try to establish theoretically whether or not music is capable of representing a specific feeling. The question must be answered in the negative, since the specification of feelings cannot be separated from actual representations and concepts, which latter lie beyond the scope of music. On the contrary, music can, with its very own resources, represent most amply a certain range of ideas.

These, corresponding to the organ which receives them, are simply all those ideas which relate to audible changes in strength, motion, and proportion; and consequently they include our ideas of increasing and diminishing, acceleration and deceleration, clever interweavings, simple progressions, and the like. Moreover, it would be possible for the aesthetical expression of a piece of music to be called charming, soft, impetuous, powerful, delicate, sprightly. These are pure ideas which have their corresponding sensuous manifestation in musical tonal relationships. So we can apply these adjectives to music without regard to their ethical significance, which has a way of becoming insidiously confused with purely musical qualities.

The ideas which the composer produces are first and foremost purely musical ideas. To his imagination there appears a particular beautiful melody. It exists for no other purpose than simply to be itself. However, just as every actual phenomenon points to the generic concept or idea which includes it, and this in turn to the idea which includes it, and so on higher and higher to the concept of the absolute Idea, so it is with musical ideas. Thus, for example, this calm adagio, harmoniously dying away, will bring the general idea of calm harmoniousness to the beautiful phenomenon. Imagination, which gladly refers artistic ideas to the peculiarly human inner awareness, will interpret this dying away on a higher level, e.g., as the expression of mellow resignation by a person of equable disposition, and can perhaps ascend instantly to an intimation of everlasting bliss in the world beyond.

Likewise, the literary and visual arts produce first of all something actual. The picture of a flower girl can indeed only indirectly suggest the general notion of girlish contentment and innocence, or a picture of a snow-covered churchyard the idea of earthly transitoriness. With music, however, the situation is different. It is only with highly questionable and arbitrary interpretations that the listener can dredge up from one piece of music the idea of youthful contentment or from another the idea of transitoriness. But these abstract ideas are not the content of the musical work, any more than they are the content of the aforementioned pictures. It is altogether impossible to speak of a musical representation of the feeling of transitoriness or of the feeling of youthful contentment.

There are ideas which can be perfectly represented by means of music and yet not occur as feeling, just as, conversely, a similar mixture of feelings could stir us emotionally but have no corresponding representation by means of a musically portrayable idea. What, then, from the feelings, can music present if not their content? Only that same dynamic mentioned above. It can reproduce the motion of a physical process according to the prevailing momentum: fast, slow, strong, weak, rising, falling. Motion is just one attribute, however, one moment of feeling, not feeling itself. It is generally accepted that music's representational capability is satisfactorily defined when we assert that it can signify not the particular object of a feeling, but rather the feeling itself, e.g., not the person loved, but rather Love. But in fact music can do the one as little as the other. It can depict not love but only such motion as can occur in connection with love or any other affect, which however is merely incidental to that affect. Love is an abstract idea, like Virtue and Immortality. The assurance of theoreticians that music cannot represent abstract ideas is superfluous: No art can do this. It goes without saying that only ideas, i.e., activated concepts, are the content of artistic embodiment,* but also that instrumental music cannot represent the ideas of love, anger, fear, because between those ideas and beautiful combinations of musical tones there exists no necessary connection. Then which moment of these ideas is it that music knows how to seize so effectively? The answer: motion. (This is, of course, "motion" in the wider sense, which also includes the increasing or decreasing of single notes or chords.) Motion is the ingredient which music has in common with emotional states and which it is able to shape creatively in a thousand shades and contrasts. The concept of motion has up to now been conspicuously neglected in investigations of the nature and effects of music. It seems to us the most important and fruitful concept.

Whatever else in music seems to portray specific states of mind is symbolic. That is to say, tones, like colours, possess symbolic meanings intrinsically and individually, which are effective apart from and prior to all artistic intentions. Every colour has its own unique character. It is not a mere cipher which has solely just such employment as the artist gives it but is a power which is by nature already in a mysterious connection with certain mental states. Who does not know the colour symbols and how they usually in their simplicity or by more subtle minds are raised to poetic refinement? We connect green with the feeling of hope, blue with loyalty. Rosenkranz recognizes graceful dignity in orange, hypocritical amiability in violet, etc. (Psychologie, 2. Aufl. S. 102.)[3]

---

*Vischer (Ästh. §11 Anmerkung) defines definite ideas as "the realms of life," insofar as their actuality may be thought of as corresponding to their concept. For the idea always points to the pure, self-sufficient concept given in its actuality.[2]

It is the same with the basic ingredients of music: different tonalities, chords, and timbres have their own characters. We are inclined to interpret these all too industriously; Schubart's key symbolism is in its way a counterpart to Goethe's interpretation of colours. Yet these ingredients (i.e., tones and colours) follow laws entirely different in their artistic application from the laws of their effects as isolated phenomena. No more than every bit of red in an historical painting means joy or every bit of white means innocence will every bit of A-flat major in a symphony arouse an ecstatic mood or every bit of B minor a misanthropic one or every triad satisfaction or every diminished seventh despair. At the aesthetical level, all such rudimentary differentiations are neutralized through subordination to higher principles. Such intrinsic connectedness is far removed from expression or representation. We call it "symbolic" because it does not directly represent the content, but it is symbolization of an entirely different order. If we see jealousy in yellow, cheerfulness in G major, mourning in cypress, of course these interpretations have a psychophysiological connection with the definiteness of these feelings – but only in our interpretations, not in the colour, the tone, or the plant in themselves. We therefore can say of a single chord neither that it represents a specific feeling nor that it does this within the artwork as a whole. Music has no other means of fulfilling its alleged purpose than the analogy between motion and the symbolism of the tones.

Granted that music's inability to represent specific feelings follows readily from the nature of the tones, it seems almost inconceivable that this has not in the course of events more rapidly achieved general acceptance. Let anyone whose heartstrings are made to resonate by a piece of instrumental music try to demonstrate with plain arguments what affect constitutes its content. The test is essential. Let us listen, for example, to Beethoven's "Prometheus" overture. What the attentive ear of the music lover hears, in continuous sequence, is something like the following: The tones of the first bar, following a descent of a fourth, sprinkle quickly and softly upward, repeating exactly in the second. The third and fourth bars carry the same upward motion further. The drops propelled upward by the fountain come rippling down so they may in the next four bars carry out the same figure and the same configuration. So there takes shape before the mind's ear of the listener a melodic symmetry between the first and second bars, then between these and the next two, and finally between the first four bars as a single grand arch and the corresponding arch of the following four bars. The rhythmically pronounced bass marks the beginning of the first three bars with a single beat, of the fourth with two beats, and it is the same with the following four bars. Here, then, is a difference between the fourth bar and the first three: The first four are by repetition symmetrical with the second four bars, so the ear is delighted by a touch of equilibrium between new and old. The harmonization of the melody shows further the correspondence of the large and the small arches: The C major triad of the first four bars corresponds to the four-two chord in the fifth and sixth bars, then to the six-five chord in the seventh and eighth. This reciprocal correspondence between melody, rhythm, and harmony produces a symmetrical yet richly varied structure which maintains still richer lights and shadows by means of the timbres of the various instruments and the fluctuations in intensity.

etc.

Beyond this we cannot by any means discern any further content in the theme or, at any rate, anything we might call a feeling which it represents or must arouse in the hearer. Such an analysis, of course, makes a skeleton out of a flourishing organism; it is apt to destroy all beauty but also at the same time all misguided interpreting.

As with this randomly selected passage, so it goes with all instrumental music. A large group of music lovers considers it to be an exclusive characteristic of the older, so-called "classical" music, that it is averse to the feelings, and concedes straight away that nobody can point to a feeling in any of J. S. Bach's preludes and fugues of the *Well-Tempered Clavier* which is its content. This distinction is equally dilettantish and arbitrary. It can be explained by the fact that in older music the autonomy appears more obvious, the interpretability more difficult and less tempting. And it proves that music does not necessarily arouse feelings and have feelings as its content. Otherwise the whole realm of figural music would go out the window. However, if important historically and aesthetically well-founded art genera have to be ignored in order sneakily to preserve a theory,* then that theory is false. It only takes a leak to sink a ship, but anyone for whom that is too slow can always smash out the bottom. He may play a theme from any symphony by Mozart or Haydn, an adagio of Beethoven, a scherzo by Mendelssohn, or a piano piece by Schumann or Chopin. These are in the mainstream of our most substantial music. Or he may play the most popular themes from overtures by Auber, Donizetti, Flotow. Who will come forward and venture to declare that some specific feeling is the content of one of these themes? One person will say "love." Possibly. Another thinks "yearning." Perhaps. A third feels "piety." Nobody can refute any of them. And so it goes. Can we call it the representation of a specific feeling when nobody knows what feeling was actually represented? Concerning the beauty of the pieces of music, probably everyone will agree. Yet concerning the content of music, everyone differs. To represent, however, is to produce a clear and distinct content, to put it before our very eyes (*darstellen – daher stellen*). How, then, can we designate something as what an art represents, when the very dubious and ambiguous elements of that art themselves are perpetually subject to of debate?

We have deliberately chosen instrumental music for our examples. This is only for the reason that whatever can be asserted of instrumental music holds good for all music as such. If some general definition of music be sought, something by which to characterize its essence and its nature, to establish its

---

*Bachians such as Spitta, to be sure, struggle with this obliquely in that, instead of disputing the theory itself in support of their master, they play Bach's fugues and suites with as voluble and delightful an outpouring of feeling as only a very subtle Beethovenian could do with his master's sonatas. This is at least consistent!

boundaries and purpose, we are entitled to confine ourselves to instrumental music. Of what *instrumental music* cannot do, it ought never be said that *music* can do it, because only instrumental music is music purely and absolutely. Whether, for its value and effects, one prefers vocal or instrumental music – an unscientific procedure prompted by the most dilettantish dogmatism – one will always have to grant that the concept "music" does not apply strictly to a piece of music composed to a verbal text. In a piece of vocal music, the effectiveness of tones can never be so precisely separated from that of words, action, and ornamentation as to allow strict sorting of the musical from the poetical. Where it is a matter of the "content" of music, we must reject even pieces with specific titles or programs. Union with poetry extends the power of music, but not its boundaries.*

*Gervinus carried further the struggle for supremacy between vocal and instrumental music in his "Händel und Shakespeare" (1868). He considers vocal music to be the only genuine and true music and instrumental music to be an altogether inferior form of art, merely a physical means to a physiological stimulus. He thereby demonstrates, with much expenditure of sagacity, nothing more than that a person can be a learned Handel enthusiast and yet proclaim a lot of strange nonsense concerning the essence of music.[4]
     Nobody has refuted these errors as strikingly as Ferdinand Hiller, from whose critique of Gervinus we take the following:

> The combinations of words with tones are of the most diverse kinds. From the simplest, half-spoken recitative to a chorus of Bach or an operatic finale of Mozart, there is a tremendous range of possible combinations. Not only in music of the recitative type, be it a separate recitative or a passage or even just an exclamation in the middle of a song, can words and music take hold of the listener with equal force. Whenever music takes the stage in all its splendour, it leaves the almighty word far behind. Proof, alas, is all too near at hand. The most tawdry poem, set to beautiful music, is powerless to diminish our pleasure in it; but the greatest poetical masterpiece cannot prop up a sagging musical work. Consider the slight interest we take in the libretto of an oratorio when we read it. One can scarcely believe that it could provide the basis of an hour of music, satisfying to the ear, heart, and soul, by a great composer. What is more, it is in most cases not at all possible for the hearer to grasp words and melody simultaneously. The conventional sounds out of which is compounded a sentence in speech must be rather quickly connected in order to be assembled in memory and grasped by the understanding. But music grips the hearer from the first tone and carries him along, without allowing him the time or even the possibility to go back over what he has heard . . .

Hiller continues:

> We can listen attentively to the simplest folksong and then to Handel's Hallelujah Chorus sustained by a thousand voices; in the former, it is the charm

In a vocal composition, we have an amalgam so perfectly fused that it would be impossible to assay any of its individual constituents. If we were dealing with the effects of poetry, it would not occur to anyone to bring up opera as the example; it requires a greater disavowal, but just the same insight, to do the same with the basic determinations of musical aesthetics.

In vocal music, the music adds colour to the black-and-white design of the poem.* We have recognized, among the ingredients of music, colours of great splendour and delicacy, which in addition possess symbolical significance. Perhaps these could transform a mediocre poem into a fervent manifestation of feeling. Yet it is not the tones which are represented in a song, but the text. The drawing, not the colouring, determines the represented content.

We appeal to the listener's capacity for abstraction. Take any dramatically

---

of a barely opened melodic flower and, in the latter, it is the power and magnificence of the combined elements of the whole realm of musical sounds by which we are charmed or enraptured. That in the one case the words are about a sweetheart and in the other about heaven contributes nothing to the primary and immediate reality. This is a purely musical essence, and it is present even if we do not understand the words or could not.

(Aus dem Tonleben unserer Zeit. Neue Folge. Leipzig 1871. S. 40 ff.)[5]

*This familiar metaphorical expression we may accept as applicable here, so long as it avoids any aesthetical claims and is a question merely of the abstract relation of music to verbal texts in general and, with it, of the decision as to which of these two factors turn out to be the autonomous, regulative determinant of the content (subject). But as soon as it is no longer a matter of the what but of the how of musical achievement, the expression of course ceases to apply. Only in a logical (we almost said juridical) sense is the text the main thing and the music a mere accessory; the aesthetical demand on the composer is much higher: It calls for autonomous musical beauty (although of course appropriate to the text). Thus, if the question is not the more abstract one of what music does when it is set to verbal texts, but rather of how in actual instances it should do so, we may not impose upon music such a dependence upon poetry as does the draughtsman upon the colourist. Ever since Gluck, in the great, inevitable reaction against the melodic encroachments of the Italians, took a retrograde step not above the happy medium but below it (exactly as did Richard Wagner in our own time), his proclamation in the dedication to *Alceste* has been incessantly parroted, that the text is the correct and well-designed drawing for which it is the sole business of music to provide the colour. If music does not interact with the poem in a much more splendid sense than as mere colouring, if it (being itself a synthesis of design and colour) does not bring in something new which recreates the words as a mere trellis upon which to climb and spread its own beautiful foliage, then it has achieved at best the status of an academic exercise or a dilettante's delight but not by any means the heights of art.

effective melody. Form a mental image of it, separated from any association with verbal texts. In an operatic melody, e.g., one which had very effectively expressed anger, you will find no other intrinsically psychical expression than that of a rapid, impulsive motion. The same melody might just as effectively render words expressing the exact opposite, namely, passionate love.

When Orpheus' aria *"Che farò senza Euridice!"* (*"J'ai perdu mon Euridice, Rien n'égale mon malheur!"*) moved thousands (including J.-J. Rousseau) to tears, Boyé, a contemporary of Gluck, remarked that one could just as well or, indeed, much more faithfully set the opposite words to the same tune (*"J'ai trouvé mon Euridice, Rien n'égale mon bonheur!"*).

Here is the beginning of the aria, with a piano reduction of the accompaniment, but with the vocal part exactly as in the Italian original:

We are, indeed, not quite sure that the composer is entirely to be absolved in this case, insofar as music certainly possesses far more specific tones for the expression of passionate grief. But we select this example out of hundreds, first, because it concerns the composer [Gluck] to whom has been attributed the greatest exactitude in dramatic expression and, second, because over the years so many people have admired in this melody the feeling of intense grief which it expresses in conjunction with those words.

But even far more specific and expressive passages of vocal music will, when separated from their texts, at best only allow us to guess which feelings they express. They are like silhouettes whose originals we cannot recognize without someone giving us a hint as to their identity.

What was true here of an isolated instance turns out to be even more true of musical enterprises of greater and the greatest scope. Many whole vocal pieces have used different texts with the same music. If someone were to present the music of, say, Meyerbeer's *The Huguenots* with different words, setting, time, characters, and incidents as *The Ghibellines in Pisa,* no doubt the ineptitude of such a revision would irritate us, but the purely musical expression would suffer not in the least. And yet the religious feeling, the evangelical fervour, which directly shapes the plot-line of *The Huguenots* would be deleted from *The Ghibellines.* (Luther's chorale does not here count as an objection to what we are saying; it is merely a quotation and would, regarded merely as music, be suitable for the enunciation of any religious doctrine.) Has the reader never heard the fugato from the overture to *The Magic Flute* performed as a vocal quartet of quarrelsome Jewish shopkeepers? Mozart's music, with not a single note altered, suits the low-comedy words almost alarmingly well, and we must laugh at the comedy just as heartily as we enjoy the seriousness of the music in the opera house. Countless testimonials of this kind can be produced, showing the adaptability of all musical motives and human feelings. The feeling of religious devotion has rightly been held up as one of the least likely to be musically misconstrued. Yet, in countless German provincial churches, the organ plays Proch's "Alphorn"[6] or the concluding aria from *La Somnambula* (with its leap of a tenth "into my arms")[7] or the like during the celebration of the Mass. Every German who goes to Italy hears with astonishment the latest popular operatic tune of Rossini, Bellini, Donizetti, and Verdi in church. These and even worldlier pieces, if they are made to sound a little bit bland, do not at all disturb the devotions of parishioners. On the contrary, people are much edified by them. If the music in itself, however, were capable of representing devotion as its content, such a quid pro quo would be impossible, rather as if the preacher recited from the pulpit a novel by Tieck or a page of parliamentary transactions instead of his sermon. Our greatest masters of sacred music, Handel in particular, offer abundant examples in support of what we are saying here. He proceeded in this with great nonchalance. Winterfeld has shown that many of the most famous pieces in *Messiah,* including some of the ones most admired for their godly sentiments, are for the most part transcribed from the secular and mainly erotic duets which Handel composed in 1711-12 for Princess Caroline of Hanover to madrigal texts by Mauro Ortensio. The second of these duets has these words:

> Nò, di voi non vo' fidarmi
> Cieco amor, crudel beltà;
> Troppo siete menzognere
> Lusinghiere deità!*

Handel used the music, unchanged in key and melody, for his chorus "For unto us a Child is born" in Part I of *Messiah.* The third sentence of this same duet, "Sò per prova i vostri inganni," has the same tune as the chorus "All we like sheep have gone astray" in Part II of *Messiah.* And from Part III, the duet "O Death, where is thy sting?" is essentially the same as the sixteenth of these madrigals, a duet for soprano and alto, of which here is the text:

> Si tu non lasci amore
> Mio cor, ti pentirai,
> Lo so ben io![8]

In J. S. Bach's music, there are numerous examples; we need only mention all the madrigal-like pieces in the *Christmas Oratorio* which, as everyone knows, were innocently transcribed from altogether dissimilar secular cantatas. And Gluck, who, as we have been taught, achieved the summit of dramatic truth in his music only by fitting each note precisely to the specific situation, indeed by tracing in his melody the very cadence of the verse, in *Armida* transcribed no fewer than five pieces from his earlier Italian operas. (See my *Moderne Oper,*

---

*"No, I will not trust you,/blind love, cruel beauty,/you are too deceitful,/flattering deity!"

p. 16.)⁹ We see that vocal music, whose theory can never determine the essence of music, is moreover in practice not in a position to give the lie to principles derived from the concept of instrumental music.

The proposition we are challenging has furthermore so permeated the flesh and blood of the view prevailing in musical aesthetics, namely that all theories derived from and related to this view rejoice in the same unimpeachability. The theory of the imitation of visible or nonmusically audible objects by music is part of that prevailing view. We are forever being solemnly reassured, when the question of "tone-painting" arises, that music cannot by itself in any way portray phenomena which lie outside its own domain, excepting only the feelings which are produced in us by music. However, it is exactly the other way around. Music can aspire to imitate only the external phenomenon, never the specific feeling it produces. The fall of snowflakes, the flutter of birds, the rising of the sun – these I can paint musically only by analogy, by producing audible impressions dynamically related to them. In pitch, intensity, tempo, and the rhythm of tones, the ear offers itself a configuration whose impression has that analogy with specific visual perception which different sense modes can attain among themselves. Just as physiologically there is a substituting of one sense for another up to a certain limit, so also aesthetically there is a certain substituting of one sense impression for another. Aesthetically there is in vogue a well-grounded analogy between motion in space and motion in time, between the colour, quality, and size of an object and the pitch, timbre and intensity of a tone. Thus one can in fact portray an object musically. But to want to portray in tones the feelings which falling snow, a crowing rooster, or flashing lightning produce in us is just ridiculous.

Although, to the best of my recollection, all musical theoreticians implicitly follow and build on the principle that music can represent specific feelings, a correct intuition keeps many of them from acknowledging it directly. The lack of conceptual definiteness in music disturbs them and leads them to modify their principle as follows: Music arouses and represents, not perhaps specific, but rather unspecific feelings. Speaking more rationally, one can only mean by this that music should embody the motion of feeling, abstracted from the content itself, i.e., from what is felt. This we have called the dynamics of feeling and have entirely conceded it to music. This ingredient of music, however, is not a representation of unspecified feelings. The terms *unspecific* and *representation* are contradictory. Mental motions as motions pure and simple, with no content, cannot be a subject for artistic embodiment, because there is no way of taking hold of them without answering questions about what moves or what is moved. That which is correct in the proposition, namely, the implied support of the view that music should not portray specific feelings, is a purely negative moment. But what is it that is positive and creative in the musical artwork? An unspecified feeling as such is not a content. If an art were to take possession of it, then the main question would still be: How is it formed? However, every artistic activity consists in individualizing, in impressing the specific upon the unspecific, the particular upon the universal. The "unspecific-feeling" theory insists upon the exact opposite. We are even worse off with this than with the previous theory, according to which we are expected to believe that music represents something, but we know not what. From here it is an easy step to the realization that music cannot represent feelings at all, either specific or unspecific. Yet what musician would have surrendered this ancient piece of his art's established territory?*

Our result perhaps still leaves room for the view that the representation of specific feelings is an ideal for music which it can never quite achieve, but which it can and should constantly strive to approach. The many grandiloquent phrases about the tendency of music to shatter the bounds of its indeterminateness and to become actual speech, the popularity of compositions in which people observe this tendency – or think they do – is evidence of how widespread this view really is.

But even more emphatically than we opposed the possibility of musical representation of feelings do we intend to oppose the view that this could ever serve as the aesthetical principle of music.

Even if it were possible for feelings to be represented by music, the degree of beauty in the music would not correspond to the degree of exactitude with which the music represented them. Let us for the moment, however, suppose that it is possible and consider the practical consequences.

Obviously we can try this fiction, not with instrumental music, which automatically excludes the evidence of specific feelings, but only with such vocal music as befits the accentuations of the mental states indicated by the text.†

Here the words in front of the composer determine the object to be portrayed. Music has the power to animate the object, to comment, and to

*To what absurdities this false principle leads, to discover in each piece of music the representation of a specific feeling, and the still falser principle that for each specific musical form there is a specific feeling as its necessary content – all this one can learn from the works of such ingenious people as Mattheson. Faithful to his basic hypothesis that we must above all establish for each melody an emotion, he tells us that a courant should express hope, a sarabande awe, a concerto grosso voluptuousness, a chaconne satiety, and an overture magnanimity (in his "Vollkommene Kapellmeister," S. 230 ff.).[10]

†The author (along with other critics who are basically in agreement) in writing criticisms of vocal music often, for the sake of brevity and convenience, innocently uses such words as "express," "portray," "represent" in connection with tones and the like. One may properly so use them, provided one remains clearly aware of their impropriety, that is, of their inadequacy with regard to symbolic and dynamic expression.

bestow upon it in greater or lesser degree the expression of individual subjectivity. It does this as far as possible through the characteristics of motion and through exploitation of the inherently symbolic aspects of tones. If it is kept in mind that the main consideration is the text and not its own distinctive beauty, then music can raise the text to higher individualization, indeed to splendour. In this case, however, the music would actually represent the feeling which already existed irremovably in the words, although capable of being enhanced. This tendency achieves in its effect something similar to the so-called representation of a feeling as the content of the particular piece of music. Granting that this actual and that supposed power of music were in fact one and the same, that the representation of feelings was possible and was the content of music, then to be consistent we would have to say that the most nearly perfect compositions were those which solved the problem most specifically. But who does not know works of utmost beauty which have no such content? (We recall the preludes and fugues of J. S. Bach.) Opposed to these there are vocal compositions which try to portray a specific feeling with the greatest accuracy, within the limits we have just explained, and in which truth of portrayal has precedence over any other principle. Upon closer examination, the outcome is that even the most relentless fitting of music to feeling in such a musical portrait generally succeeds in inverse proportion to the autonomous beauty of the music and therefore that declamatory-dramatic exactitude and musical perfection go only halfway together, and then they go their ways separately.

Recitative shows this most clearly, being that type of music which most directly fits its own declamatory expression to the accentuation of individual words, attempting no more than to be a faithful imitation of specific, usually rapidly changing states of mind. This must, as the true embodiment of the feeling-theory, be the noblest and most perfect music. In fact, however, in recitative, music is reduced to the status of a handmaiden and loses its autonomous significance. This is proof that the expression of specific mental processes does not coincide with the purpose of music but, on the contrary, in the last analysis is obstructively opposed to music. Suppose we perform a long recitative, omitting the words, and then ask what is its musical value and meaning. All music to which we are supposed to ascribe the effect produced must undergo this test, however.

By no means do we have to limit ourselves to recitative. In the highest and most advanced artforms, we can find confirmation that musical beauty is constantly disposed to yield to specific expressions, because the former demands an autonomous content and the latter a self-abnegating servitude.

Let us move upward from the declamatory principle in recitative to the dramatic in opera. The music of Mozart's operas is in complete accord with its text. If we listen without text even to the most complicated sections of these, i.e., the finales, the middle voices will remain somewhat indistinct, but the principal voices and total effect will be beautiful music. As everyone knows, to satisfy in due proportion the musical and dramatic requirements is considered to be the ideal of opera; this ideal itself is nevertheless for this very reason a constant struggle between the principle of dramatic realism and that of musical beauty, with endless compromises between the two. So far as I know, this has never been discussed to any great extent. That it is untrue that every character in an opera has a singing role is not what makes the theoretical principle of opera problematical and troublesome – such illusions enter the imagination with great ease – but the constraint which forces music and text into continually overstepping and yielding results in opera's being, like a constitutional government, based on the constant tension between two legitimate rival parties. This struggle, in which the artist must allow sometimes one and sometimes the other to triumph, is the point from which all the inadequacies of opera originate. And all rules of art which would prescribe dogmatically just for opera have failed. It follows that the musical and dramatic principles must necessarily intersect. If the two lines are long enough, however, they will seem to the human eye parallel for a considerable distance.

Something similar holds of dance, as can be seen in any ballet. The more it abandons the beautiful rhythmicity of its forms, in order to become eloquent gestures and mimicry to express specific thoughts and feelings, the more it approaches the crude significance of mere pantomime. The enhancement of the dramatic principle in dance produces a corresponding violation of its plastic and rhythmic beauty. Similarly, an opera can never be the same sort of thing as a spoken drama or a piece of instrumental music. So the aim of a good opera composer will be at least a constant reconciling and adjusting, never a favouring of the one aspect over the other. In doubtful cases, however, he will decide in favor of the musical claims, since opera is first of all music, not drama. We can easily assess this claim by means of the peculiar, very different expectations with which we go to a dramatic or an operatic treatment of the same subject. Neglect of the musical component will always be strikingly evident.*

*What Mozart said about the position of music vis-à-vis poetry in opera is highly characteristic of him. Wholly in opposition to Gluck, who would have music subordinate to poetry, Mozart took the view that poetry should be the obedient daughter of music. In opera he assigns to music, wherever it is associated with the expression of feeling, the authority to decide. He relies on the fact that good music is forgiving to the most wretched texts (it would be difficult to find an instance of the opposite); but Mozart's view follows undeniably also from the essence and character of music. Yet, because music directly and more potently than any other art seizes and lays claim totally upon the senses, music causes the impression, which the poetic expression makes by verbal means, to recede temporarily. Furthermore, it influences the imagination and the feelings through the sense of hearing in an as yet apparently unexplained manner with a power to stimulate which likewise momentarily surpasses poetry. (O. Jahn, "Mozart," III. 91).[11]

The famous controversy between Gluck's followers and those of Piccini is historically significant because it was the first time there was extensive discussion of the inner conflict of opera due to the opposition of the two factors, the musical and the dramatic. Of course this occurred without a scholarly awareness of the immense theoretical significance of the outcome. Whoever makes the worthwhile effort to trace this musical controversy back to its origins* will observe there how in the richly varied scale between insolence and flattery there prevails the altogether facetious gladiatorial adroitness of French polemic, but along with it such a meagre comprehension of the basic issues, such a lack of solid learning, that for musical aesthetics no result emerges from this long-drawn-out debate. The major participants, Suard and Abbé Arnaud for Gluck, Marmontel and La Harpe against, repeatedly went beyond Gluck's critique to an elucidation of the dramatic principles in opera and its relation to the musical. However, they treated this relation as if it were one characteristic of opera among others, not as the innermost vital principle. They had no idea that the whole existence of opera depends upon the verdict over this relation. It is noteworthy how closely Gluck's opponents particularly agreed on the point from which the error of the dramatic principle could be perfectly beheld and overthrown. LaHarpe wrote as follows in the *Journal de Politique et de la Littérature* of 5 October 1777:

> One may object that it is not natural to sing a song of this kind in an emotionally excited situation, that to burst into song is to stop the action and to nullify the dramatic effect. I find these objections absolutely illusory. To begin with, if we are going to have singing at all, we must have the most beautiful possible singing, and it is not more natural to sing badly than to sing well. All the arts are founded on conventions, on the given. When I go to the opera, it is to listen to the music. I do not overlook the fact that Alceste did not make her farewell to Admetus while singing an aria, but, since Alceste is in the theatre to sing, if I recognize her sadness and her love in a melodious aria, then I enjoy her song while being interested in her misfortune.[13]

Can one doubt that La Harpe failed to see how splendidly he stood on firm ground? For it almost immediately occurs to him to object to the duet between Agamemnon and Achilles in *Iphigenia* because it is entirely inconsistent with the dignity of these two heroes that they should speak at the same time. With this he forsook and betrayed that firm ground, the principle of musical beauty, and implicitly, indeed unconsciously, accepted the principle of the opposition. The more consistently we seek to keep unadulterated the dramatic prin-

---

*The most important of these polemical treatises are to be found in the collection "Mèmoires pour servir a l'histoire de la Révolution opérée dans la musique par Mr. le chevalier Gluck." Naples et Paris 1781.[12]

ciple in opera, withholding from it the life's breath of musical beauty, the more sickly it becomes, like a bird in a vacuum jar. We must necessarily return to the pure spoken drama, wherein we at least have the proof that opera is really impossible, so long as we do not admit supremacy in opera to the musical principle (while fully aware of its incompatibility with reality). In actual artistic practice, even this truth has never been denied. Gluck himself, the most rigorous dramatist, laid down the false principle that operatic music is nothing more than heightened declamation. In practice, however, the inborn musicality of the man comes through, always to the great benefit of his works. The same applies to Richard Wagner. In the present connection, we need only mention that Wagner's main thesis, which he enunciates in the first volume of *Opera and Drama,* rests on a false basis: "The mistake of opera as an art genre lies in this, that a means (music) is made an end, but this end (drama) is made a means."[14] This is false because an opera in which the music is always and actually used as a means for dramatic expression would be a musical monstrosity.*

---

*I cannot forbear quoting here a few appropriate remarks of Grillparzer and M. Hauptmann.

"It is absurd," says Grillparzer, "to make the music in an opera into a mere slave of the poetry," and he continues:

> If the music in the opera is there only to express once again what the poet had already expressed, then get rid of the music. . . . Whosoever knows thy power, Melody, which, with no need of words, from heaven through the human breast to heaven thou again returnest; whosoever knows thy power will not make thee handmaiden of poetry: He will prefer to give precedence to the latter (and I believe poetry deserves precedence as does manhood over childhood), but he will also concede to the former its own independent realm, and regard both as siblings and not as lord and servant or guardian and ward.

He will hold firmly to the maxim: "No opera should be considered from the point of view of poetry – from this all dramatic musical composition is nonsense – but rather from the point of view of music."
Another passage from Grillparzer reads:

> For no opera composer is it easier to fit the music precisely to the words than it is for the composer who puts his music together in a mechanical fashion. On the other hand, he whose music possesses organic life, an internally grounded necessity, readily comes into collision with the words. That is to say, every genuine melodic theme has its own inner law of formation and development, which to the real musical genius is sacred and inviolable, and which he cannot relinquish just to satisfy the words. The musical prosaist can start and stop anywhere, because bits and pieces are easily lifted from one

One consequence (among others) of the Wagnerian claim regarding means and ends would be that all composers have committed a serious error so long as they tried to compose better than mediocre music to mediocre texts and plots and that we likewise commit a serious error when we enjoy such music.

The union of poetry with music and opera is a morganatic marriage. The more closely we look at this union, into which musical beauty enters with its specifically dictated content already waiting for it, the more illusory its indissolubility seems to us.

How does it happen that in every song we can make many small alterations which, without in the least weakening the expression of feeling, yet immediately destroy the beauty of the musical themes? This would be impossible if the latter were dependent upon the former. And how does it happen that many

---

place and put down in some other, but anyone who has a sense of wholeness can only either wholly produce or wholly let be. This is not meant to advocate negligence toward the text, but in isolated cases it should exonerate, indeed justify, such negligence. That is why Rossini's puerile trifling is nevertheless worth more than Mosel's prosaic intellectual posturing, which damages the essence of music in order to follow the empty stammerings of the poet. That is why we can often accuse Mozart of offences against the libretto, but Gluck never. That is why this much extolled characteristic of music is frequently a very negative virtue, that it usually limits itself so that joy is expressed by nonsadness, grief by noncheerfulness, gentleness by nonharshness, anger by nongentleness, love by flutes, and despair by trumpets and kettledrums with contrabasses. The composer must be faithful to the plot, not to the words. When he comes across something outstanding in his music, he must always ignore the libretto.

In these aphorisms, written decades ago, is there not much that sounds like a polemic against Wagner's theories and the *Walküre* style? Grillparzer takes a penetrating look at the audience with this remark: "Those who demand a purely dramatic effect from an opera are usually those who also want a musical effect from a dramatic poem, i.e., a purely arbitrary effect." IX, 144 ff.[15]

Similarly M. Hauptmann to O. Jahn:

To me (when listening to the operas of Gluck) it was as if the composer's intention was to be true, but not musically true, only verbally true, and this is not infrequently musically false. Words are by their nature clipped, but music wants to taper off. Music is always the vowel to which words are merely the consonants, and only the vowel can have the accent, being what sounds and never merely that which sounds by means of something else. Yet one always hears music, however verbally true it may be, also for itself. Therefore it must also be listened to for itself.

(Briefe an Spohr u., ed. F. Hiller. Leipzig 1867. S. 106)[16]

songs which flawlessly express their text seem to us intolerably bad? From the standpoint of the feeling-theory, there is no way around this.

What remains, then, as the principle of beauty in music, now that we have rejected the feeling theory as inadequate?

A completely other, autonomous factor, which we shall proceed at once to examine.

III

THE MUSICALLY BEAUTIFUL

So far we have proceeded negatively and have sought merely to refute the erroneous assumption that the beauty of music has its being in the representation of feeling. To that sketch, we now have to fill in the positive content. This we shall do by answering the question: What kind of beauty is the beauty of a musical composition?

It is a specifically musical kind of beauty. By this we understand a beauty that is self-contained and in no need of content from outside itself, that consists simply and solely of tones and their artistic combination. Relationships, fraught with significance, of sounds which are in themselves charming – their congruity and opposition, their separating and combining, their soaring and subsiding – this is what comes in spontaneous forms before our inner contemplation and pleases us as beautiful.

The primordial stuff of music is regular and pleasing sound. Its animating principle is rhythm: rhythm in the larger scale as the co-proportionality of a symmetrical structure; rhythm in the smaller scale as regular alternating motion of individual units within the metric period. The material out of which the composer creates, of which the abundance can never be exaggerated, is the entire system of tones, with their latent possibilities for melodic, harmonic, and rhythmic variety. Unconsumed and inexhaustible, melody holds sway over all, as the basic form of musical beauty. Harmony, with its thousandfold transformations, inversions, and augmentations, provides always new foundations. The two combined are animated by rhythm, the artery which carries life to music, and they are enhanced by the charm of a diversity of timbres.

If now we ask what it is that should be expressed by means of this tone-material, the answer is musical ideas. But a musical idea brought into complete manifestation in appearance is already self-subsistent beauty; it is an end in itself, and it is in no way primarily a medium or material for the representation of feelings or conceptions.

28

The content of music is tonally moving forms.[1]

How music is able to produce beautiful forms without a specific feeling as its content is already to some extent illustrated for us by a branch of ornamentation in the visual arts, namely arabesque. We follow sweeping lines, here dipping gently, there boldly soaring, approaching and separating, corresponding curves large and small, seemingly incommensurable yet always well connected together, to every part a counterpart, a collection of small details but yet a whole. Now let us think of an arabesque not dead and static, but coming into being in continuous self-formation before our eyes. How the lines, some robust and some delicate, pursue one another! How they ascend from a small curve to great heights and then sink back again, how they expand and contract and forever astonish the eye with their ingenious alternation of tension and repose! There before our eyes the image becomes ever grander and more sublime. Finally, let us think of this lively arabesque as the dynamic emanation of an artistic spirit who unceasingly pours the whole abundance of his inventiveness into the arteries of this dynamism. Does this mental impression not come close to that of music?

As children, all of us have much enjoyed the play of colour and shape in a kaleidoscope. Music is a kind of kaleidoscope, although it manifests itself on an incomparably higher level of ideality. Music produces beautiful forms and colours in ever more elaborate diversity, gently overflowing, sharply contrasted, always coherent and yet always new, self-contained and self-fulfilled. The main difference between such a musical, audible kaleidoscope and the familiar visible one is that the former presents itself as the direct emanation of an artistically creative spirit, while the latter is no more than a mechanically ingenious plaything. If, not merely in thought but in actuality, we want to raise colour to the level of music, we get involved in the tasteless frivolity of colour organs and the like. The invention of these devices, for all that, does at least show how the formal aspects of both music and colour rest on the same basis.

If some sensitive music lover objects that our art is degraded by analogies such as the above, we reply that it is not much to the point whether the analogy is precise or not. We do not degrade a thing by becoming better acquainted with it. If we want to relinquish the attribute of motion, of sequential development, for which the example of the kaleidoscope is particularly apt, we can of course find a loftier analogy for the musically beautiful in architecture, in the human body, or in a landscape, which likewise have a primitive beauty of outline and colour (setting aside the soul, the spiritual expression).

If people do not acknowledge the abundance of beauty residing in the purely musical, one may blame the undervaluation of the sensuous, which we find in the older systems of aesthetics favouring morality and aesthetic sensitivity and in Hegel's system favouring the "Idea." Every art originates from and is active within the sensuous. The feeling theory fails to recognize this; it ignores hearing entirely and goes directly to feeling. Music creates for the heart, they say; the ear is of no consequence. Indeed, for what they call the ear, namely the labyrinth or the eardrum, no Beethoven composes. The auditory imagination, however, which is something entirely different from the sense of hearing regarded as a mere funnel open to the surface of appearances, enjoys in conscious sensuousness the sounding shapes, the self-constructing tones, and dwells in free and immediate contemplation of them.

It is extraordinarily difficult to describe this specifically musical, autonomous beauty. Since music has no prototype in nature and expresses no conceptual content, it can be talked about only in dry technical definitions or with poetical fictions. Its realm is truly not of this world. All the fanciful portrayals, characterizations, circumscriptions of a musical work are either figurative or perverse. What in every other art is still description is in music already metaphor. Music demands once and for all to be grasped as music and can be only from itself understood and in itself enjoyed.

In no way is the specifically musically beautiful to be understood as mere acoustical beauty or as symmetry of proportion – it embraces both as ancillary – and still less can we talk about an ear-pleasing play of tones and other such images, by which the lack of a mental source of animation tends to become emphasized. Thus, in order to make our case for musical beauty, we have not excluded ideal content but, on the contrary, have insisted on it. For we acknowledge no beauty without its full share of ideality. Basically what we have done is to transfer the beauty of music to tonal forms. This already implies that the ideal content of music is in the most intimate relationship with these forms. In music the concept of "form" is materialized in a specifically musical way. The forms which construct themselves out of tones are not empty but filled; they are not mere contours of a vacuum but mind giving shape to itself from within. Accordingly, by contrast with arabesque, music is actually a picture, but one whose subject we cannot grasp in words and subsume under concepts. Music has sense and logic – but musical sense and logic. It is a kind of language which we speak and understand yet cannot translate. It is due to a kind of subconscious recognition that we speak of musical "thoughts," and, as in the case of speech, the trained judgment easily distinguishes between genuine thoughts and empty phrases. In the same way, we recognize the rational coherence of a group of tones and call it a sentence,[2] exactly as with every logical proposition we have a sense of where it comes to an end, although what we might mean by "truth" in the two cases is not at all the same thing.

The gratifying reasonableness which can be found in musical structures is based upon certain fundamental laws of nature governing both the human organism and the external manifestations of sound. It is mainly the law of harmonic progression (an analogue to the circle in the visual arts) which produces the nucleus of the most significant musical development and the explanation (itself unfortunately almost inexplicable) of the various musical relationships.

All musical elements have mysterious bonds and affinities among themselves, determined by natural laws. These, imperceptibly regulating rhythm, melody, and harmony, require obedience from human music, and they stamp as caprice and ugliness every noncompliant relationship. They reside, though not in a manner open to scientific investigation, instinctively in every cultivated ear, which accordingly perceives the organic, rational coherence of a group of tones, or its absurdity and unnaturalness, by mere contemplation, with no concept as its criterion or *tertium comparationis.**

This negative, intrinsic rationality is inherent in the tonal system by natural law. In it is grounded the further capacity of tones for entering into the positive content of the beautiful.

Composing is a work of mind upon material compatible with mind. This material is immensely abundant and adaptable in the composer's imagination, which builds, not like the architect, out of crude, ponderous stone, but out of the aftereffects of audible tones already faded away. Being subtler and more ideal than the material of any other art, the tones readily absorb every idea of the composer. Since tonal connections, upon the relationships of which musical beauty is based, are achieved not through being linked up mechanically into a series, but by spontaneous activity of the imagination, the spiritual energy and distinctiveness of each composer's imagination make their mark upon the product as character. Accordingly, as the creation of a thinking and feeling mind, a musical composition has in high degree the capability to be itself full of ideality and feeling. This ideal content we demand of every musical artwork. It is to be found only in the tone-structure itself, however, and not in any other aspect of the work. Concerning the place of ideality and feeling in a musical composition, our view is to the prevailing view as the notion of immanence is to that of transcendence.

Every art has as its goal to externalize an idea actively emerging in the

---

*Of course, poetry is to some extent able to make use of the ugly (unbeautiful), in which case the effect of poetry upon feeling is due entirely to the concepts which poetry evokes directly. Thus the concept of appropriateness will mitigate the impression of ugliness to such an extent that ugliness (the unbeautiful) can elicit the grandest effects. But the impression of music will be received and enjoyed directly from sensation; the understanding's approval comes too late to compensate for the intrusion of the ugly. Hence Shakespeare can go all the way to the hideous, but Mozart has to stay within the limits of the beautiful.

(Grillparzer, IX. 142.)[3]

artist's imagination. In the case of music, this idea is a tonal idea, not a conceptual idea which has first been translated into tones. The starting point of all the creative activity of the composer is not the intention to portray a specific feeling but the devising of a particular melody. Through this deep-seated, mysterious power, into the workings of which the human eye will never penetrate, there resounds in the mind of the composer a theme, a motive. We cannot trace this first seed back to its origins; we have to accept it simply as given. Once it has occurred in the composer's imagination, his activity begins, which, starting from this principle theme or motive and always in relation to it, pursues the goal of presenting it in all its relationships. The beauty of a self-subsistent, simple theme makes itself known in aesthetical awareness with an immediacy which permits no other explanation than the inner appropriateness of the phenomenon, the harmony of its parts, without reference to any external third factor. It pleases us in itself, like the arabesque, the ornamental column, or like products of natural beauty such as leaves and flowers.

Nothing could be more misguided and prevalent than the view which distinguishes between beautiful music which possesses ideal content and beautiful music which does not. This view has a much too narrow conception of the beautiful in music, representing both the elaborately constructed form and the ideal content with which the form is filled as self-subsistent. Consequently this view divides all compositions into two categories, the full and the empty, like champagne bottles. Musical champagne, however, has the peculiarity that it grows along with the bottle.

One particular musical conception is, taken by itself, witty; another is banal. A particular final cadence is impressive; change two notes, and it becomes insipid. Quite rightly we describe a musical theme as majestic, graceful, tender, dull, hackneyed, but all these expressions describe the musical character of the passage. To characterize this musical expressiveness of a motive, we often choose terms from the vocabulary of our emotional life: arrogant, peevish, tender, spirited, yearning. We can also take our descriptions from other realms of appearance, however, and speak of fragrant, vernal, hazy, chilly music. Feelings are thus, for the description of musical characteristics, only one source among others which offer similarities. We may use such epithets to describe music (indeed we cannot do without them), provided we never lose sight of the fact that we are using them only figuratively and take care not to say such things as "This music portrays arrogance," etc.

Detailed examination of all the musical determinations of a theme convinces us, however, that, despite the inscrutableness of the ultimate ontological grounds, there is a multitude of proximate causes with which the ideal expression of a piece of music is in precise correlation. Each individual musical element (i.e., each interval, tone-colour, chord, rhythmic figure, etc.) has its own characteristic physiognomy, its specific mode of action. The artist is inscrutable, but the artwork is not. One and the same melody will not sound the same when accompanied by a triad as when accompanied by a chord of the sixth. A melodic interval of a seventh is wholly unlike a sixth. The accompanying rhythm of a motive, whether loud or soft, on whatever kind of musical instrument, modifies the motive's specific colouration. In brief, each individual factor in a musical passage necessarily contributes to its taking on its own unique ideal expression and having its effect upon the listener in this way and no other. What makes Halévy's music bizarre and Auber's charming, what brings about the peculiarities by which we at once recognize Mendelssohn and Spohr, can be traced to purely musical factors without reference to the obscurities of the feelings.

Why Mendelssohn's numerous six-five chords and narrow diatonic themes, Spohr's chromaticisms and enharmonic relations, Auber's short, bipartite rhythms, etc., produce just these specific, unequivocal impressions: These questions, of course, neither psychology nor physiology can answer.

If, however, we are asking about proximate causes (and this is a matter of importance especially in connection with the arts), the powerful effect of a theme comes not from the supposed augmentation of anguish in the composer but from this or that augmented interval, not from the trembling of his soul but from the drumstrokes, not from his yearning but from the chromaticism. The correlation of the two we shall not ignore; on the contrary, we shall soon examine it more closely. We should keep in mind, however, that scientific examination of the effect of a theme can only be done with those aforementioned invariable and objective data, never with the supposed state of mind which the composer externalizes by means of them. If we want to reason from that state of mind directly to the effects of the work or to explain the latter in terms of the former, we might perhaps arrive at a correct conclusion but will have omitted the most important thing, the middle term of the syllogism, namely, the music itself.

The proficient composer possesses a working knowledge, be it more by instinct or by deliberation, of the character of every musical element. Nevertheless, a theoretical knowledge of these characters, from their most elaborate constructions to the least discriminable element, is required for scientific explanation of the various musical effects and impressions. The particular feature by which a melody has its power over us is not merely some kind of obscure miracle of which we can have no more than an inkling. It is rather the inevitable result of musical factors which are at work in the melody as a particular combination of those factors. Tight or broad rhythm, diatonic or chromatic progression, each has its characteristic feature and its own kind of appeal. That is why a trained musician, from a printed account of an unfamiliar composition, will get a much better idea of it if he reads, for example, that diminished sevenths and tremolos predominate, than from the most poetical description of the emotional crisis through which the reviewer went as a result of listening to it.

Investigation of the nature of each separate musical element and its connection with a specific impression (just of the facts of the matter, not of the ultimate principles) and finally the reduction of these detailed observations to general laws: that would be the philosophical foundation of music for which so many authors are yearning (without, incidentally, telling us what they really understand by the expression "philosophical foundation of music"). The psychological and physical effect of each chord, each rhythm, each interval, however, is by no means explained by saying that this is red, the other green, this is hope, the other discontent, but only by subsuming the particular musical qualities under general aesthetical categories and these in turn under a supreme principle. If, in the former manner, the separate factors were explained in their isolation, it would then have to be shown how they determine and modify each other in their various combinations. Most musically learned people have granted to harmony and contrapuntal accompaniment the preeminent position as the ideal content of a composition. In making this claim, however, they have proceeded much too superficially and atomistically. Some people have settled upon melody as the prompting of genius, as the vehicle for sensuousness and feeling (the Italians are famous for this); harmony has been cast opposite melody in the role of vehicle for the genuine content, being learnable and the product of deliberation. It is curious the way people keep going along with such a superficial way of looking at things. There is basic truth in both claims, but neither at this level of generality nor in isolation do they carry weight. The mind is a unity, and so is the musical creation of an artist. A theme emerges fully armed with its melody and its harmony, together, out of the head of the composer. Neither the principle of subordination nor that of opposition applies to the essence of the relation of harmony to melody. Both can in one place pursue their own lines of development and in another place readily subordinate one to the other. In either case, the highest degree of ideal beauty can be achieved. Is it perhaps the (very sketchy) harmony in the principle themes of Beethoven's "Coriolanus" overture and Mendelssohn's "Hebrides" which confers upon them the expression of brooding melancholy? Would Rossini's "Oh, Matilda" or a Neapolitan folksong achieve more spirit if a basso continuo or a complicated chord sequence replaced the sparse harmonic background? Each melody must be thought up along with its own particular harmony, with its own rhythm and sonority. The ideal content is due only to the conjunction of them all; mutilation of any one part damages also the expression of the remainder. That melody or harmony or rhythm should be able to predominate is to the advantage of all, and to consider on the one hand all genius to be in chords, and on the other all triviality to be in the lack of them, is sheer pedantry. The camellia blooms without scent; the lily, without colour; the rose delights us with both colour and scent. These qualities cannot be transferred from one to another, yet each of the blossoms is beautiful. So the "philosophical foundation of music" would have to try first of all to find out which necessary ideal determinants are connected with each musical element, and in what manner they are connected. The double requirement of a strictly scientific framework and the most elaborate casuistics makes the task a very formidable but not quite insurmountable one: to strive for the ideal of an "exact" science of music after the model of chemistry or of physiology.

The manner in which the creative act takes place in the mind of the composer of instrumental music gives us the most reliable insight into the nature of musical beauty. A musical idea simply turns up in the composer's imagination; he elaborates it. It takes shape progressively, like a crystal, until imperceptibly the form of the completed product stands before him in its main outlines, and there remains only to realize it artistically, checking, measuring, revising. The composer of a piece of instrumental music does not have in mind the representation of a specific content. If he does this, he places himself at a wrong standpoint, more alongside music than within it. His composition becomes the translation of a program into tones which then are unintelligible without the program. We neither deny nor underestimate the conspicuous talent of Berlioz if we mention his name here. Liszt has emulated him with his much feebler "symphonic poems."

Just as out of the same marble one sculptor carves ravishing forms, the other clumsy botchings, so the musical scales in different hands take on the form of a Beethoven overture or one by Verdi. What makes the difference between these two compositions? That the one represents a heightened emotion, perhaps, or the same emotion more faithfully? No, rather that it is constructed in more beautiful tone-forms. This alone makes a piece of music good or bad, that one composer puts in a theme sparkling with genius, the other a commonplace one; that the former works everything out in new and significant relationships, while the latter always makes his (if anything) worse. The harmony of the one unfolds eventually and with originality, while that of the other turns out to be not so much flawed as impoverished; the rhythm in the one throbs with life; in the other, it thumps like a military tattoo.

There is no art which wears out so many forms so quickly as music. Modulations, cadences, intervallic and harmonic progressions all in this manner go stale in fifty, nay, thirty years, so that the gifted composer can no longer make use of them and will be forever making his way to the discovery of new, purely musical directions. Without inaccuracy we may say, of many compositions which were outstanding in their own day, that once upon a time they were beautiful. Out of the primordially obscure connections of musical elements and their innumerable possible combinations, the imagination of the gifted composer will bring to light the most elegant and recherché. It will construct tone-forms which appear to be devised out of free choice yet are all necessarily linked together by an imperceptible, delicate thread. Such works or details we do not hesitate to call works of genius. With this we can easily correct Oulibicheff's mistaken opinion that a piece of instrumental music cannot be a product of genius because "genius in a composer consists purely and simply in a certain applicability of his music to a direct or indirect program."[4] According to our view, it would be entirely correct to say that the famous D-sharp in the Allegro of the *Don Giovanni* overture or the descending unisons in the same is a stroke of genius. But, contrary to Oulibicheff's view, the former has never represented Don Giovanni's misanthropy and never will, nor has the latter the fathers, husbands, brothers, and lovers of the women seduced by the Don.[5] All such interpretations are objectionable in themselves, but they become doubly so with regard to Mozart, who is the greatest musical genius in history: Everything he touched was transformed into music. Oulibicheff also sees the G minor symphony as the story of a passionate love affair told in exactly four instalments.[6] But the G minor symphony is music and nothing more, and anyway that is enough. We do not look for representations of specific mental processes or events in music, but above all else for music itself, and we enjoy purely what it gives completely. If the musically beautiful is missing, it will never be compensated for by cooking up some great meaning. And such a meaning is superfluous if the musically beautiful is present. In any case, it totally misrepresents the musical conception. The people who would claim for music a place among the revelations of the human soul – a place which it does not have and can never achieve, because it is incapable of imparting beliefs – those very people have also brought into vogue the term "intention." In music no amount of "intention" can replace invention. Whatever does not become outwardly apparent is, so far as music is concerned, altogether nonexistent, but whatever has become apparent has ceased to be mere intention. The expression "He has intentions," which is for the most part used with approval, seems to me more like a reproach which, in plain language, goes like this: "The artist would like to do great things, but he is incapable of it." Art, however, derives from capability. Whoever lacks capability has nothing but "intentions."

Like its beauty, the laws of the construction of a piece of music are grounded exclusively in its musical determinants. Concerning this there are many fluctuating and absurd views, of which we will bring up only one here. This is precisely the view arising out of the generally accepted idea of sonata and symphony which comes from the feeling theory. According to this view, the composer has to represent four separate and distinct states of mind which, in the separate movements of the sonata, must nevertheless together be a coherent whole (how?). In order to justify the undeniable coherence of the movements and to explain the different impressions they make upon us, we in effect compel the listener to impute to them specific feelings as their content. The explanation is sometimes appropriate, more often not, and never is it so by necessity. But this will always occur by necessity: that four musical movements which mutually contrast and enhance one another, according to musical-aesthetical laws, are combined into a single whole. We are indebted to the highly imaginative painter M. von Schwind for a very attractive illustration of the Fantasia for Piano op. 80 by Beethoven.[7] The artist has grasped the separate movements as interrelated events involving the same central characters and has represented them pictorially. Just as the painter extracts scenes and figures from the tones, so does the listener classify them as feelings and events. Both interpretations have some kind of connection with the tones, but not a *necessary* one. And scientific laws have to do only with necessary connections.

It is often said that Beethoven, while sketching many of his compositions, must have thought of specific events or states of mind. Where Beethoven or any other composer followed this procedure, he used it merely as a device whereby the coherence of an external event makes it easier to keep hold of the musical entity. If Berlioz, Liszt, etc., believed they got more than this out of the poem, the title, or the experience, this was a self-delusion. It is the unity of musical impression which characterizes the four movements of a sonata as organically unified, not the connection with objects thought of by the composer. Where such poetical leading-strings as these are denied and purely musical ones devised, there we will find no other unity of the parts than a musical unity. Aesthetically it is a matter of indifference whether Beethoven had to adopt such specific subjects even for all his compositions; we do not know what they were, hence so far as the work is concerned they do not exist. Apart from all interpretation, it is the work itself which is under consideration. And as the jurist pretends that whatever is not in the evidence is not in the world, so for aesthetic judgment nothing is available which is not in the work of art. If the parts of a composition appear unified to us, this unity must have its basis in musical determinants.*

---

*These lines have scandalized Beethoven "experts" such as Lobe,[8] to mention only one. We can do no better than answer them with the following comments of Otto Jahn in his essay concerning the new Beethoven edition of Breitkopf & Härtel ("Ges. Aufsätze über Musik"). His comments are in complete accord with our views.

Jahn refers to Schindler's famous statement that Beethoven, being asked about the meaning of his D minor and F minor sonatas, replied: "Just read Shakespeare's *The Tempest*." "Presumably," says Jahn,

the questioner will get from the reading of the play the firm convinction that Shakespeare's *The Tempest* does not have the same effect on him as it did on

Finally we shall head off a possible misunderstanding by investigating our concept of the musically beautiful according to three of its facets.

The musically beautiful, in the specific meaning we have adopted, is not limited to music in the so-called "classical" style, nor does it include a preference for the classical over the romantic. It applies to the one as to the other: to Bach as well as Beethoven, to Mozart as well as Schumann. So our thesis contains no hint of partisanship. The whole drift of the present inquiry avoids questions of what ought to be and considers only what is. From this it deduces no particular musical ideal as the only genuine beauty but merely establishes in the same way for all schools what the beautiful is in each, even the most antagonistic.

It is only recently that people have begun looking at artworks in relation to the ideas and events of the times which produced them. In all likelihood this undeniable connection also applies to music. Being a manifestation of the

---

Beethoven and in him produces no sonata in D minor or F minor. That this particular drama could prompt Beethoven to compose such works is certainly not without interest, but to claim to get an understanding of them from Shakespeare betrays an incapacity for musical comprehension.

Beethoven is supposed to have had the tomb scene in *Romeo and Juliet* in mind while composing the Adagio of his F minor quartet (op. 18, no. 1). But if someone were to reread this scene attentively and then listened to the Adagio in order to visualize the scene, would his enjoyment of the music be increased or hindered?

Titles and program notes, even if based on information stemming from Beethoven himself, would not help us penetrate to the essential meaning and significance of the art work. . . . it is much more to be feared that they would be just as likely to cause misunderstandings and perversities as those which Beethoven published. The beautiful sonata in E-flat major (op. 81), as everyone knows, has the title "Les adieux, l'absence, le retour" and is accordingly regarded as an authentic example of program music. "One may surmise that these are episodes in the life of a loving couple," says Marx, setting aside the question of whether the lovers were married or not, "but the composition itself provides the proof." Of the conclusion to the sonata Lenz says: "The lovers spread their arms as migratory birds spread their wings." It is the case that Beethoven wrote on the original score of the first section: "Farewell on the occasion of the departure of His Imperial Highness Archduke Rudolf, May 4, 1809." And he wrote on the second section: "Arrival of His Imperial Highness Archduke Rudolf, January 30, 1810. . . . " Just think how Beethoven would have resisted the suggestion that he had portrayed the Archduke's amorous wing-flappings at the end of the piece!

"So we can be satisfied," concludes Jahn, "that even Beethoven did not as a rule utter such words, which would only have misled too many people into the error that whoever understands the title understands the artwork. Beethoven's music says *everything* he wanted to say."[9]

human mind, it must, of course, also stand in interrelation with the other activities of mind: with contemporaneous productions of the literary and visual arts, the poetic, social, scientific conditions of its time, and ultimately with the individual experiences and convictions of the composer. The examination and demonstration of this interrelation are therefore warranted with regard to individual composers and works, and they are truly profitable. Yet we must always keep in mind that drawing such a parallel between artistic matters and special historical circumstances is an art-historical and not at all an aesthetical procedure. While the connection between art history and aesthetics seems necessary from the methodological point of view, yet each of these two sciences must preserve unadulterated its own unique essence in the face of unavoidable confusion of one with the other. The historian, interpreting an artistic phenomenon in its wider context, might see in Spontini the expression of the French Empire period, in Rossini the political restoration. The aesthetician, however, has to limit himself exclusively to the works of these men, to inquire what in these works is beautiful and why. Aesthetical inquiry does not and should not know anything about the personal circumstances and historical background of the composer; it hears and believes only what the artwork itself has to say. It will accordingly discover in Beethoven's symphonies (the identity and biography of the composer being unknown) turbulence, striving, unappeasable longing, vigorous defiance; but that the composer had republican sympathies, was unmarried and becoming deaf, and all the other features which the art historian digs up as illuminating it will by no means glean from the works and may not be used for the evaluation of them. To compare differences in world view between Bach, Mozart, and Haydn and then go back to the differences between their compositions may count as a very attractive and meritorious exercise, yet it is infinitely complicated and will be the more prone to fallacies, the stricter the causal connection it seeks to establish. The danger of exaggeration as a result of accepting this principle is extraordinarily great. We can all too easily interpret the most incidental contemporary influence as a matter of inherent necessity and interpret the perpetually untranslatable language of music any way we like. It is purely on account of quick-witted delivery that the same paradox spoken by a clever person sounds like wisdom but, spoken by a simple person, sounds like nonsense.

Even Hegel, in discussing music, often misled in that he tacitly confused his predominantly art-historical point of view with the purely aesthetical and identified in music certainties which music itself never possessed. Of course there is a connection between the character of every piece of music and that of its author, but for the aesthetician this is not open to view. The idea of necessary connection between all phenomena can in its actual application be exaggerated to the point of caricature. Nowadays it takes real heroism to declare, in opposition to this pleasantly stimulating and ingeniously represented

trend, that historical comprehension and aesthetical judgment are two different things.* It is objectively certain, first, that the variety of impressions of
the various works and schools is based upon crucially dissimilar arrangements
of the musical elements, and second, that what rightly pleases in a composition,
be it the strictest fugue of Bach or the dreamiest nocturne of Chopin, is
musically beautiful.

Even less than with the classical can the musically beautiful be equated
with the architectonic, which includes the musically beautiful as one of its
branches. The rigid grandeur of superimposed towering figurations, the elaborate entwining of many voices, of which none is free and independent, because
all of them are – these have their own ageless rightness. Yet those marvellously
sombre vocal pyramids of the old Italians and Netherlanders are just one small
part of the realm of the musically beautiful, just as are the many exquisitely
wrought saltcellars and silver candelabra of the venerable Sebastian Bach.

Many aestheticians consider that musical enjoyment can be adequately
explained in terms of regularity and symmetry. But no beauty, least of all
musical beauty, has ever consisted entirely in these. The most insipid theme
can be constructed with perfect symmetry. *Symmetry* is merely a relational
concept; it leaves open the question: What is it, then, that appears symmetrical?
Orderly structure may be detected among the trivial, shabby fragments of even
the most pathetic compositions. The musical sense of the word demands
always new symmetrical creations.†

---

*If we mention in this connection *Musikalischen Charakterköpfe* by Riehl, it is with
grateful acknowledgment of this brilliant and stimulating book.[10]

†I permit myself to quote here from my book *Die Moderne Oper* by way of illustration.

The well-known saying that the "truly beautiful" can never lose its charm, even
after a long time, is for music little more than a pretty figure of speech. (And
anyway, who is to be the judge of what is "truly beautiful"?) Music is like
nature, which every autumn lets a whole world of flowers fall into decay, out
of which arise new flowerings. All music is the work of humans, product of a
particular individuality, time, culture, and is for this reason permeated with
mortal elements of various life-expectancies. Among the great musical forms,
opera is the most complex and conventional and therefore the most transitory.
It may be saddening that even the most excellent and brilliant new operas
(such as those of Spohr and Spontini) are already beginning to disappear from
the theatres. But reality is indefeasible, and the process cannot be halted by
blaming the evil spirit of the time, as people have always done. Time is itself a
spirit, and it produces its own embodiment. In contrast to the study place of
the silent score-reader, the operatic stage is the forum for the actual demands
of the public. The stage symbolizes the life of drama, and the struggle for its
possession is drama's struggle for existence. In this struggle, a trifling work

Most recently Oersted has expounded this Platonic view in connection with music by means of the example of the circle, for which he claims positive beauty.[12] We may suppose that he had no firsthand experience of such an atrocity as an entirely circular composition.

Perhaps more out of caution than from need, we may add in conclusion that the musically beautiful has nothing to do with mathematics. This notion, which laymen (sensitive authors among them) cherish concerning the role of mathematics in music, is a remarkably vague one. Not content that the vibrations of tones, the spacing of intervals, and consonances and dissonances can be traced back to mathematical proportions, they are also convinced that the beauty of a musical work is based on number. The study of harmony and counterpoint is considered a kind of cabala which teaches compositional calculus.

Even though mathematics provides an indispensable key for the investigation of the physical aspects of musical art, its importance with regard to completed musical works ought not to be overrated. In a musical composition, be it the most beautiful or the ugliest, nothing at all is mathematically worked out. The creations of the imagination are not sums. All monochord experiments, acoustic figures, proportions of intervals, and the like, are irrelevant: The domain of aesthetics begins where these elementary relationships, however important, have left off. Mathematics merely puts in order the rudimentary material for artistic treatment and operates secretly in the simplest relations. Musical thought comes to light without it, however. I confess that I do not understand it when Oersted asks: "Would the lifetime of several mathematicians be enough to calculate all the beauties of a Mozart symphony?"* What is there that should or can be calculated? Perhaps the ratio of the vibrations of each tone with those of the next or the lengths of individual phrases or

---

quite frequently overcomes its betters if it conveys to us the breath of our time, the heartbeat of our sentiments and desires. The public, like the artist, has a legitimate inclination toward the new in music, and criticism which has admiration only for the old and not also the courage to recognize the new undermines artistic production. We must renounce our belief in the deathlessness of the beautiful. Has not every age proclaimed with the same misguided confidence the imperishability of its best operas? Yet Adam Hiller declared in Leipzig that if ever the operas of Hasse ceased to delight, general anarchy must ensue. And yet Schubart, the music-aesthetician from Hohenasperg, assured us concerning Jomelli that it was unthinkable that this composer could ever fall into oblivion. And who today ever heard of Hasse and Jomelli?

(Vorwort S. vi.)[11]

*"Geist in der Natur," 3. Band, deutsch von Kannegießer. S. 32.[13]

sections with relation to each other? What makes a piece of music a work of art and raises it above the level of physical experiment is something spontaneous, spiritual, and therefore incalculable. In the musical artwork, mathematics has just as small or great a share as in the productions of the other arts. For ultimately mathematics must also guide the hand of the painter and sculptor; mathematics is involved in the measures of verses, in the structures of the architect, and in the figures of the dancer. In every precise study, the application of mathematics, as a function of reason, must find a place. Only we must not grant it an actual, positive, creative power, as so many musicians and aesthetical conservatives would cheerfully have it. Mathematics is in a way like the production of feelings in the listener: It occurs in all the arts, but only in the case of music is a big fuss made about it.

Likewise some people have frequently drawn a parallel between speech and music and have tried to lay down the laws of the former as the laws of the latter. The kinship of song with speech is close enough that one might go along with the similarity of physiological conditions or with their common characteristics as revealing the inner self through the human voice. The analogical relationships are so striking that there is no need for us to go into the matter here. So we would just grant explicitly that, wherever music actually deals just with the subjective revealing of an inner longing, the laws governing speech will in fact to some extent be decisive for song.

That the person who gets into a rage raises the pitch of his voice, while the voice of a speaker who is recovering his composure descends; that sentences of particular gravity will be spoken slowly, and casual ones quickly: These and their like the composer of songs, particularly of dramatic songs, ignores at his peril. However, some people have not been content with these limited analogies but consider music itself to be a kind of language (though more unspecific or more refined), and now they want to abstract the laws of its beauty from the nature of language and trace back every attribute and effect of music to its affinity with language. We take the view that, where the specifics of an art are concerned, their differences with regard to respective domains are more important than their similarities. Such analogies are often enticing but are not at all appropriate to the actual essence of music. Undistracted by them, aesthetical research must push unrelentingly on to the point where language and music part irreconcilably. Only from this point will the art of music be able to germinate truly fruitful aesthetical principles. The essential difference is that in speech the sound[14] is only a sign, that is, a means to an end which is entirely distinct from that means, while in music the sound is an object, i.e., it appears to us as an end in itself. The autonomous beauty of tone-forms in music and the absolute supremacy of thought over sound as merely a means of expression in spoken language are so exclusively opposed that a combination of the two is a logical impossibility.

The essential centre of gravity thus lies entirely differently in language and music, and around these centres all other characteristics arrange themselves. All specifically musical laws will hinge upon the autonomous meaning and beauty of the tones, and all linguistic laws upon the correct adaptation of sound to the requirements of expression.

The most harmful and confused views have arisen from the attempt to understand music as a kind of language; we see the practical consequences every day. Above all, it must seem appropriate to composers of not much creative power to regard autonomous musical beauty (which to them is inaccessible) as a false, materialistic principle and to opt for the programmatic significance of music. Quite apart from Richard Wagner's operas, we often come across interruptions in the melodic flow of even the most insignificant instrumental pieces, due to disconnected cadences, recitatives, and the like. These startle the hearer and behave as if they signify something special, but in fact they signify nothing but ugliness. Some people have taken to praising modern compositions which keep breaking up the overall rhythm and developing inexplicable bumps and heaped-up contrasts. Thus they would have music strive to burst forth from its narrow limits and elevate itself to speech. To us this kind of commendation has always seemed equivocal. The limits of music are by no means narrow, but they are very precisely drawn. Music can never be "elevated" to the level of speech (strictly speaking, from the musical standpoint, one must say "lowered"), since music obviously would have to be an elevated kind of speech.*

---

*It will not have gone unnoticed that one of the most original and magnificent works of all time has, by virtue of its splendor, contributed to the well-beloved fiction of modern music criticism about "the craving of music's inner self for the definiteness of verbal speech" and "the casting aside of the fetters of the harmonic proportions in sound." We refer to Beethoven's Ninth Symphony. It is one of those spiritual watersheds which interpose themselves insuperably between opposing currents of conviction.

For some musicians, the grandeur of "intention," the spiritual significance of the abstract purpose, comes ahead of everything else. Such musicians place the Ninth Symphony at the summit of all music, while the few who, clinging to the unfashionable view of beauty, struggle on behalf of purely aesthetical claims, are a bit restrained in their admiration. As may be guessed, the problem is mainly with the Finale, since, concerning the sublime (though not flawless) beauty of the first three movements, little disagreement will arise among attentive and competent listeners. In this last movement, we have never been able to see more than the vast shadow of a titanic body. That from lonely despair a soul is brought in joy to reconciliation is a thought whose immensity a person could understand perfectly while yet finding the music of the last movement (for all its brilliance) unbeautiful. We know all too well the universal disapprobation which attaches to so heterodox a view. One of the most gifted and versatile of German scholars, who in the "A. Allgemeinen Zeitung" (1853) undertook to challenge the formal analysis of the Ninth Symphony, acknowledged for this reason the comical

Even our singers forget this, who in deeply moving passages bellow words, indeed phrases, as if speaking them, and believe they have thereby demonstrated the highest degree of intensification of music. They fail to notice that the transition from singing to speaking is always a descent, so that the highest normal tone in speech sounds even deeper than the deepest sung tone of the same voice. Just as bad as these practical consequences, indeed worse, because they cannot be experimentally refuted, are theories which would foist upon music the laws of development and construction of speech, as had been attempted in earlier times by Rousseau and Rameau and more recently by the disciples of R. Wagner. The true heart of music, the formal beauty which gratifies in itself, would thereby be pierced through, and the chimera of "meaning" pursued. An aesthetics of musical art must therefore take as its most important task to set forth unrelentingly the basic distinction between the essence of music and that of language and in all deductions hold fast to the principle that, where the specifically musical is concerned, the analogy with language does not apply.

---

necessity of identifying himself in the title as a "numskull." He directed attention to the aesthetical monstrosity involved in having a multimovement instrumental work end with a chorus and compared Beethoven to a sculptor who carved the legs, torso, and arms of a figure out of colourless marble and then coloured the head. Presumably at the entry of human voices every sensitive listener must be overcome by the same discomfort, "since here the work shifts its centre of gravity with a jolt, and thereby threatens to knock the listener down." Almost a decade later, to our delight, the "numskull" was unmasked and turned out to be David Strauss.[15]

On the other hand, the estimable Dr. Becher, who may here be considered the representative of a whole school of thought, said, concerning the fourth movement, in an essay about the Ninth Symphony published in 1843: "With regard to originality of form, as well as magnificence of composition and the bold sweep of individual conceptions, it is a product of Beethoven's genius not at all to be compared with any other existing musical work." He declares that for him this movement, "with Shakespeare's *King Lear* and perhaps a dozen other manifestations of the human spirit, towers in its immense poetical power above those other artistic peaks like a Dhaulāgiri among the Himalayas." Like almost all his kindred spirits, Becher gives a detailed account of the meaning of the "content" of each of the four movements and their deep symbolism, but of the music, he has nothing to say.[16] This is utterly characteristic of a whole school of music criticism which, in reply to the question of whether the music is beautiful or not, prefers to sidestep into a solemn disquisition about some great thing the music is supposed to mean.

IV

ANALYSIS OF
THE SUBJECTIVE
IMPRESSION OF MUSIC

We accept as a basic principle and as the first task of musical aesthetics that it place the usurped supremacy of feeling under the legitimate authority of beauty, where not feeling but imagination (as the activity of pure contemplation) is the organ from and for which all artistic beauty comes in the first place. Yet, in practical musical life, the positive manifestations of feeling retain too conspicuous and important a role for them to be set aside on account of mere subordination.

Even though aesthetical investigation must stick to the artwork itself, this autonomous artwork turns out to be in fact an efficacious mediator between two kinetic powers, its whence and its whither, i.e., the composer and the hearer. In the psyches of these two, the artistic activity of the imagination cannot be extracted as pure metal in such a way as to be deposited in the complete, objective work. Rather it operates in their psyches always in close interrelation with feeling and sensation. Thus the feelings will retain a significance, before and after completion of the work, first in the composer and then in the hearer, from which we cannot withhold consideration.

Take first the composer. During the creative activity, an exaltation will fill him such as can scarcely be thought superfluous for the release of the beautiful from the depths of the imagination. That this exalted mood, according to the idiosyncrasy of the artist, takes on more or less the coloration of the merging artwork; that it will flow sometimes vehemently, sometimes moderately, but never with such overwhelming passion as to thwart artistic production; that lucid deliberation maintains, during all this, at least equal importance with inspiration: These are well-known rules belonging to the teaching of art in general. What concerns the creativity of the composer in particular and therefore must be kept firmly in mind is that it is a continuous shaping, a modelling in tonal relations. The supremacy of feeling, which people so readily attribute to music, seems nowhere more misplaced than where it is presupposed of the

45

composer in his creative activity, and this activity is taken to be inspired extemporizing. Initially the composer has only a vague notion of the outlines of a composition. It is chiselled, from the individual beats up to the distinctive shape of the completed work, perhaps directly into the responsive and variform orchestral guise. This labour, proceeding step by step as it does, is so deliberate and complex that nobody can be expected to comprehend it who has not so much as tried his hand at it. Not just fugal or contrapuntal movements, in which in measured fashion we sustain note against note, but also the most smoothly flowing rondo and the most melodious aria demand in minutest detail a "working out" (as the saying so aptly goes). The composer's activity is in its way plastic and comparable to the visual artist's. Just as little as the visual artist should the composer be dependently involved with his physical material, for like him the composer has his (in this case, musical) ideal to set forth objectively in order to create pure form.

This may have been overlooked by Rosenkranz when he observed but did not resolve the paradox of why women, who are by nature preeminently dependent upon feeling, have not amounted to much as composers.* The cause of this lies (apart from the circumstances in general which prevent women from achieving more in the way of intellectual creativity) precisely in the plastic aspect of musical composing, which demands renunciation of subjectivity (although in a different way) no less than the visual arts. And it is not feeling which composes music, but the specifically musical, artistically trained talent. Hence it is amusing when F. L. Schubart in all seriousness describes the "masterly andantes" of the composer Stamitz as a natural consequence of his heart's being full of feeling† or when Christian Rolle assures us that an affable, affectionate character enables us to build slow movements which are masterworks.‡

Without spiritual ardour, nothing great or beautiful has ever been accomplished in this life. In the composer (*Tondichter*), as in every poet, feeling will be found to be highly developed, only it is not the creative factor in the composer. Even when a powerful, specific emotion possesses him totally, so that it becomes the cause and inauguration of many an artwork, yet that emotion never becomes the subject of the work. This we know from the nature of musical art, which has neither the ability nor the vocation to represent a specific feeling.

*Rosenkranz, Psychologie. 2.Aufl. S.60.[1]

†Schubart, "Ideen zu einer Ästhetik der Tonkunst." 1806.[2]

‡"Neue Wahrnehmungen zur Aufnahme der Musik." Berlin 1784. S. 102.[3]

An inner singing, not a mere inner feeling, induces the musically gifted person to construct a musical artwork.

We have established that the activity of the composer is a kind of constructing; as much, it is altogether objective. The composer shapes something autonomously beautiful. The limitlessly expressive ideal material of the tones permits the subjectivity of his inner formative process to make its mark upon the products of his shaping. Since the individual musical elements already possess their own characteristic expressiveness, the predominant characteristics of the composer turn out to be such things as sentimentality, energy, serenity. These clearly reveal themselves through the composer's consistent partiality toward certain tonalities, rhythms, transitions, in accordance with the prevailing impulse which the music is able to reproduce. Once they have been absorbed out of the artistic process into the product, however, these characteristics are of interest as musical determinations, i.e., as the character of the composition, not of the composer.*

Whatever the sentimental composer produces and whatever the ingenious one, be it elegant or sublime, is music first and foremost, objective structure. Their works will differ from one another through unmistakeable idiosyncracies, and, viewed as a whole, they will reflect the individuality of their creators. Yet each and every one of them will have been created for its own sake as purely musical autonomous beauty.

It is not the actual feeling of the composer, as a merely subjective emotional state, that evokes the corresponding feeling in the hearer. If we do concede so coercive a power to music, we thereby acknowledge its cause to be something objective in the music, since only something objective can coerce in any kind of beauty. In the present instance, this something objective is the musical determinants of a particular piece. In a strictly aesthetical sense, we can say of any theme at all that it sounds noble or sad or whatever. We cannot say, however, that it is an expression of the noble or sad feelings of the composer. Even further removed from the character of a musical work as such are the social and political conditions which dominate its time. The aforementioned musical expression of the theme is a necessary consequence of its musical determinants having been selected just as they were and not otherwise. That this selection resulted from psychological or cultural-historical causes

---

*What care is necessary in drawing conclusions regarding the composition from the human character of the composer and at the same time how great is the danger that imagination influences dispassionate research to the disadvantage of truth has recently been demonstrated by (among others) the biography of Beethoven by A. B. Marx. He considered his musically prejudiced panegyric to be exempt from the need for careful research of the facts, with the result that his book has had to be drastically revised on many points in the light of Thayer's careful study of the sources.[4]

must be established by reference to the particular work (and not just from date and place of birth). And, were this connection established, however interesting it may be, it would be first and foremost an exclusively historical or biographical fact. Aesthetical contemplation cannot be based upon any features which are outside the artwork itself.

Just as the individuality of the composer will assuredly find symbolic expression in his creations, so it would be wrong to seek to derive, from this personal or subjective moment, concepts which have their true basis only in the objectivity of artistic constructions. The concept of style is one of these.*

We are inclined to understand style in the art of music, regarded from the point of view of music's specifically musical determinations, to be consummate technique as it shows itself in the expression of creative ideas as if by second nature. The master keeps up his "style," while embodying his clearly grasped idea, by omitting everything paltry, improper, and trivial, thus consistently maintaining, in every technical detail, the artistic demeanor of the whole. With Vischer (*Ästhetik* §527), we shall use the word *style* unconditionally with regard to music, and say (disregarding historical or personal categories): "This composer has style," in the sense that one says of somebody: "He has character."[6]

The question of style brings the architectonic aspect of the musically beautiful prominently to the fore. The style of a piece of music will violate a higher principle than that of mere proportion if a single bar, though in itself irreproachable, is out of keeping with the effect of the whole. Just like a misplaced piece of architectural ornamentation, a cadence or a modulation which sticks out from the otherwise consistent development of the basic artistic concept is a violation of style because it disrupts the unity of the work. Of course, this is *unity* in a wider and higher sense, which embraces contrast, episode, and many kinds of liberty.

In the act of composing a piece of music, the artist can divest himself of only as much of his personal emotional state as the limits of a predominantly objective and formal activity permit.

The act in which the direct emanation in tones of a feeling can take place is not so much the fabrication as the reproduction[7] of a musical work. That, philosophically speaking, the composed piece, regardless of whether it is performed or not, is the completed artwork ought not to keep us from giving consideration to the division of music into composition and reproduction,

---

*For this reason, Forkel's derivation of the various musical styles by "thinking of the differences" is wrong. According to his view, the style of any composer has as its basis that the visionary, arrogant, indifferent, naive, and pedantic man produces pomposity and overpowering emphasis in the connecting up of his thoughts or is standoffish and affected. (Theorie der Musik. 1777. S.23.)[5]

which is one of the most important special features of our art, wherever this division contributes to our understanding of a musical phenomenon.

It makes itself felt preeminently in the investigation of the subjective impression of music. To the performer it is granted to release directly the feeling which possesses him, through his instrument, and breathe into his performance the wild storms, the passionate fervour, the serene power and joy of his inwardness. The bodily ardour that through my fingertips suddenly presses the soulful vibrato upon the string, or pulls the bow, or indeed makes itself audible in song, in actual fact makes possible the most personal outpouring of feeling in music-making. Here a personal attitude becomes directly audibly effective in tones, not just silently formative in them. The composer works slowly and intermittently, the performer in impetuous flight; the composer for posterity, and the performer for the moment of fulfillment. The musical artwork is formed; the performance we experience. Thus the emotionally cathartic and stimulating aspect of music is situated in the reproductive act, which coaxes the electric spark out of its obscure secret place and flashes it across to the listener. Of course the performer can deliver only what is already in the composition; this demands not much more than playing the right notes. Some say that the performer has only to fathom and reveal the spirit of the composer. Fair enough. In the instant of re-creation, however, this very assimilation is the work of his, the performer's, spirit. The same piece disturbs or delights, according to how it is animated into resounding actuality, just as one and the same person is at one time seen as full of rapture, and at another time, dull and despondent. The most artistically contrived music box cannot move the hearer, yet the simplest street singer will do this if he is heart and soul caught up in his song.

The highest degree of immediacy in the musical revelation of mental states occurs where creation and performance coincide in a single act. This happens in free improvisation. Where this proceeds not with formally artistic but with predominantly subjective intent (pathological in a higher sense), the expression which the player wheedles out of the keyboard can become a kind of genuine speaking. Whoever has experienced at first hand this uncensored discourse, this reckless abandonment of the self to the grip of a powerful spell, will already know how love, jealousy, rapture, and grief come roaring, undisguised yet unbidden, out of their night, to celebrate their feasts, sing their sagas, clash in battle, until their master the player recalls them, quietened, disquieting.

We turn now to the listener, to whom the liberated activity of the one who plays communicates the expression of what is played. We often see the listener deeply stirred by a piece of music, moved to joy or melancholy, transported in his innermost being far beyond mere aesthetical pleasure, or disturbed. The existence of these effects is undeniable, actual and genuine, often reaching the greatest intensity. It is so well known that we need not tarry over it. Here we are concerned with only two of its aspects: in what way this specifically musical arousal of feeling is distinct from others and to what extent this effect is aesthetical.

Even if we have to grant to all the arts, without exception, the power to produce effects upon the feelings, yet we do not deny that there is something specific, peculiar only to it, in the way music exercises that power. Music works more rapidly and intensely upon the mind than any other art. With a few chords, we can be transported into a state of mind which a poem would achieve only through lengthy exposition, or a painting only through a sustained effort to understand it, although poetry and painting, to their advantage over music, have at their service the whole range of ideas upon which our thinking depends for its awareness of the feelings of pleasure and pain. The effect of tones is not only more rapid but more immediate and intensive. The other arts persuade, but music invades us. We experience this, its unique power over the spirit, at its most powerful, when we are severely agitated or depressed.

When we are in a state where neither paintings nor poems, statues nor buildings are any longer able to arouse our interest, music still will have power over us, indeed precisely in this circumstance more intensely than otherwise. For one who has to hear or make music while in a distressingly agitated mood, music throbs like vinegar in an open wound. The shape and character of what we hear then lose their significance entirely; be it an adagio gloomy as night or a lilting waltz, we cannot disentangle ourselves from its sounds. No longer are we aware of the piece, but only of the sounds themselves, the music as amorphous demonic power, as it acts upon the nerves of our whole body.

When Goethe at a great age came to know once again the power of love, there awakened in him at the same time a susceptibility to music such as he had never known. To Zelter he wrote concerning those miraculous days (1823) at Marienbad: "The immense power of music over me these days! The voice of Milder, the sonorities of Szymanowska, yes, and even the public concerts of the local military band, open up my heart, as one opens a clenched fist in friendly gesture. . . . I am thoroughly convinced that I would have to leave the room at the first notes from your choir." Too perceptive not to recognise the large component of nervous agitation in this manifestation, Goethe ended his letter with these words: "You would cure me of an unhealthy susceptibility which, for all that, is properly to be regarded as the cause of this phenomenon."[*] These observations must surely draw our attention to the fact that, in musical effects upon feeling, often an extraneous, not purely aesthetical element may be involved. A purely aesthetical effect addresses itself to a healthy nervous system and does not rely upon any degree of psychological abnormality.

---

[*]Briefwechsel zwischen Goethe und Zelter, 3.Band S.322.[8]

In fact the more intensive influence of music upon our nervous system supports music's claim to a superabundance of power greater than that of the other arts. But when we inquire into the nature of this superabundance, we realize that it is a qualitative one, and that its peculiar quality is based on physiological conditions. The sensuous factor, which in all aesthetic pleasure sustains the ideal, is in the case of music greater than in the other arts. Music, being the most ideal because of its nonphysical material, yet on the side of its contentless play of forms the most sensuous art, exhibits in this mysterious union of two opposites an active striving to adapt to the nerves, those no less obscure organs of the imperceptible telegraph service between body and soul.

The intensive influence of music upon the nervous system is fully accepted as fact by psychology as well as physiology. Unfortunately, an adequate explanation of this is still lacking. Psychology can by no means penetrate the mesmeric compulsion of the impression which certain chords, timbres, and melodies make upon the whole human organism, because it [i.e., the mesmeric compulsion] is first and foremost a matter of a specific stimulation of the nerves. Just as little has the triumphantly progressing science of physiology produced anything decisive concerning our problem.

Whatever the musical monographs of these hybrid sciences deal with, they almost universally tend to present music with an aura of the miraculous by holding up brilliant showpieces, rather than scientifically tracing the true and indispensable connection of music with our nervous system. But this latter is what we need, not the staunch conviction of a Doctor Albrecht, who prescribed music as a sudorific,[9] not the incredulity of Oersted, who explained the howling of a dog, in response to the sound of music in certain keys, as a result of the thrashing by which the dog had been conditioned.*

It may not be known to many music lovers that we possess an extensive literature concerning the bodily effects of music and their medical applications. Rich in interesting curiosities but untrustworthy in observation and unscientific in explanation, most of these musico-medical writings seek to raise up some very complex and incidental property of music to the status of a sovereign remedy.

From Pythagoras, who is supposed to have been the first to have accomplished miraculous cures by means of music, up to our time, the doctrine has cropped up again and again, enriched more through new examples than through new ideas, that the stimulating or alleviating effects of tones can be applied to the bodily organism as a remedy against numerous ailments. Peter Lichtenthal tells us in detail, in his *Der Musikalische Arzt*,[11] how gout,

---

*"Der Geist in der Natur." III,9.[10]

sciatica, epilepsy, catalepsy, pestilence, delirium, convulsions, the jitters, and even "stupidity" (*stupiditas*) may be cured by means of the power of tones.*

With regard to the basis of their theory these writers fall into two types. One of them argues from the body and bases the healing power of music upon the physical effects of sound waves, which pass along to the other nerves through the auditory nerve, and by means of such pervasive vibration bring about a salubrious reaction in the ailing organism. The emotional states which are at the same time observable are nothing but a consequence of this nervous vibration, since not only do passions bring about certain bodily changes, but these latter in their turn are able to produce corresponding passions.

According to this theory, to which (following the Englishman Webb) Nikolai, Schneider, Lichtenthal, J. J. Engel, Sulzer, and others adhere,[13] we are moved by music in just the same way as our windows and doors begin to vibrate when in proximity to powerful musical sounds. In corroboration are put forward such examples as Boyle's servant whose gums began to bleed when he heard a saw being sharpened[14] or the many people who develop convulsions from the sound of a knife scraping on glass.

But this is not music. That music shares the same material substratum (i.e., sound) with those manifestations in which sounds act so intensely upon the nerves will later be seen to have important consequences for us. Here we are emphasizing an antimaterialistic view, namely, that music begins where those isolated effects leave off. And, anyway, the sadness to which an adagio can reduce the listener is not at all comparable to the bodily sensation of a piercing sound.

The other half of our writers (including Kausch[15] and most aestheticians) account for the curative effects of music from the psychological point of view. They argue that music arouses feelings and passions in the soul, that feelings have among their consequences strong agitations in the nervous system, and that strong agitations in the nervous system bring about a salutary reaction in the diseased organism. This reasoning, the flaws in which do not really need to be pointed out, is so staunchly defended by this idealistic "psychological" school, against the previously mentioned materialistic, that they (the psychologists), with the Englishman Whytt[16] as their authority and in defiance of all physiology, deny that there is a connection between the auditory nerve and

---

*This doctrine achieved the peak of confusion with the famous doctor Baptista Porta, who combined the notions of medicinal plants and musical instruments and cured dropsy with a flute made of hellebore stem. A musical instrument made of poplar wood was supposed to cure sciatica; one carved out of a cinnamon stick, impotence. (Encyclopédie, article "musique.")[12]

the other nerves. According to this view, of course, any bodily transmission of an auditory stimulus to the organism as a whole will be impossible.

The conception that through music specific feelings, such as love, sorrow, anger, and rapture, are aroused in the soul, which heal the body through salutary agitation, has a convincing ring. It makes one think of the delightful verdict handed down by one of our most illustrious natural scientists, concerning the so-called "Goldberger electromagnetic chains." He said that, while we do not yet know whether an electric current can cure certain illnesses, we do know that the Goldberger chains are incapable of generating an electric current.[17] As applicable to our music therapists, what all this amounts to is that it is possible for certain emotional states to induce a turn for the better in bodily illnesses. However, it is not possible to produce on demand whatever emotional state one pleases.

The two theories, the psychological and the physiological, are similar in that both argue from questionable assumptions to even more questionable conclusions and end up in the most questionable clinical practices. It may be that logical objections could cause a therapeutic method to be discarded. It is a bit of a problem, however, that up to now no doctor has ever been known to send his typhus patients to Meyerbeer's *The Prophet* or to reach for a horn instead of the lancet.

The bodily effect of music is in itself neither so strong, nor so reliable, nor so independent of physical and aesthetical preconditions, nor, finally, so manipulable at will that it could be a possibility as an effective cure. Every cure carried out with the assistance of music has the character of an exceptional one, whose success had at no time been ascribed to the music alone but depended upon particular, perhaps entirely private, bodily and spiritual conditions. It is very noteworthy that the only application of music which can actually be found in medicine, namely, in the treatment of mental illnesses, has in view chiefly the spiritual side of musical effects. It is well known that modern psychiatry uses music in many cases and with favourable results. This is based, however, neither on the physical vibration of the nervous system nor on the arousal of the passions but on the soothingly cheerful effect which music, half distracting and half captivating, is able to exercise upon a depressed or overwrought spirit. Though the mental patient really listens to the sensuous and not the artistic aspect of the piece, yet if he listens attentively, he is no doubt at some level of aesthetical comprehension, however rudimentary.

Once it is established that an integral part of the emotional change produced by music is physical, it follows that this phenomenon, as encountered essentially in our neural activity, ought also to be investigated on this, its corporeal side. The musician can attain no scientific certainty with regard to this problem unless he makes himself acquainted with the results of contemporary physiological research on the connection of music with the feelings. If we trace the pathway which a melody must follow in order to act upon our state of feeling, we find that it goes from vibrating instrument to auditory nerve, as is made amply clear in Helmholtz's epoch-making *Lehre von den Tonempfindungen.*[18] Acoustics demonstrates in detail the external conditions under which we perceive tones generally or under which we perceive this or that particular tone. Anatomy reveals to us, with the aid of the microscope, the structure of the organs of hearing, down to the finest and most internal. And physiology, which of course can employ no direct observation in the study of this extremely small, delicate and deeply concealed, marvellous structure, has nevertheless securely established its manner of operating partly through a hypothesis so clearly elucidated that the whole process of tonal sensation is now physiologically comprehensible. Moreover, upon the area in which natural science already touches closely upon aesthetics, the researches of Helmholtz on consonance, dissonance, and tonal relationships have shed much light where until just recently there was darkness. But of course that is as far as our knowledge goes. What it would be most important to know and what remains unexplained is the neural process through which the sensation of tone becomes feeling or mood. Physiology tells us that what we experience as tone is a molecular motion in neural tissue and indeed just as much so in the central nervous system as in the auditory complex. It teaches us that the fibres of the auditory nerve are connected to the other nerves and that they transmit impulses to them and that hearing is in especially close connection with the cerebellum and cerebrum, with the larynx, lungs, and heart. What physiology does not tell us, however, is the particular way in which particular musical factors, such as chords, rhythms, and instruments, act upon different nerves. Does a musical auditory sensation communicate itself to all nerves connected with the auditory complex or to only a few? With how much intensity? By which musical elements is the brain, from which originate the nerves leading to heart and lungs, most affected? It is not to be denied that dance music brings about a twitching of the body, especially in the feet, of young people whose natural disposition is not entirely inhibited by the constraints of civilization. It would be pedantic to deny the physiological effect of marches and dance music and to seek to reduce it merely to the psychological association of ideas. What is psychological about it, namely, awakened memories and the well-known pleasure of dancing, is not lacking in explanation, but the explanation is not at all adequate. It is not because it is dance music that it lifts the foot; rather, it is because it lifts the foot that it is dance music. Anyone who glances around a bit at the opera will soon notice how, with lively, accessible melodies, the ladies automatically nod their heads this way and that, but never with an adagio, however moving or melodic. Does it follow that certain musical relationships, especially rhythmic ones, act on motor nerves, and others only on sensory nerves? When is the former the case? When the latter?* Is the solar plexus, which traditionally is regarded as one of the main loci of sensation, especially responsive to music? Are the sympathetic nerves? (Purkinje once remarked to me that, of all the nerves, these have the prettiest name.[20]) Why one sound seems shrill and disagreeable, another pure and pleasant, is explained acoustically by the uniformity and nonuniformity of successive gusts of air, and why some tones sounded together are consonant or dissonant, by regular and symmetrical or irregular and asymmetrical flow.† These explanations of more or less simple auditory sensations cannot satisfy the aesthetician. He insists upon an explanation of feeling and asks: How is it that one series of euphonious sounds gives the impression of grief, and another, equally euphonious, of joy? Whence the opposing moods, often occurring with compelling force, with which different chords or instruments of similarly pure, euphonious sound inspire the hearer?

So far as we know, physiology can answer none of these questions. And how could it? Does physiology know how grief produces tears, how joy produces laughter? In fact it does not know what grief and joy are! Therefore let everyone take care not to seek from a science explanations which it cannot give.‡

Of course the basis of every feeling aroused by music must lie first of all in a particular manner of affecting the nerves by an auditory impression. But how an excitation of the auditory nerve, which we cannot even trace to its origins, is perceived as a particular sense quality; how the bodily impression becomes a

*Carus, in his explanation of this motor stimulus, has the auditory nerve originating in the cerebellum, in which also he locates the seat of the will, and from both he derives the characteristic effects of auditory impressions upon deeds of courage and the like. But that is a very shaky hypothesis, since not even the derivation of the auditory nerve from the cerebellum is a scientifically certain fact.

Harless defends the view that mere rhythmic perception, without any auditory impression, has the same motor effect as rhythmic music, which seems to be at odds with our practical experience. (R. Wagner, Handwörterbuch der Physiologie, artikel "Hören.")[19]

†Helmholtz, Lehre von den Tonempfindungen. 2.Aufl. 1870. S.319.[21]

‡One of our most brilliant physiologists, Lotze, in his "medizinischen Psychologie" (S.237) says: "Reflection upon melodies would lead to the admission that we know nothing at all about the conditions under which a transition of the nerves from one kind of excitation to another provides a physical basis for powerful aesthetical feelings which follow the change of tones." And on the impression of pleasure and its opposite which a single tone can exert upon feeling (S. 236): "It is altogether impossible for us to assign precisely a physiological basis to these impressions of simple sensations, because the direction in which they alter neural activity is too little understood for us to derive from it the magnitude of the conduction or inhibition."[22]

mental state; finally, how sensation becomes feeling: All that lies on the other side of the mysterious divide which no investigator has crossed. There are paraphrases a thousandfold of this one ancient riddle: How the body is connected to the soul. This sphinx will never throw herself off her rock.*

What physiology has to offer the science of music is of the utmost importance for our comprehension of auditory impressions as such, but not as music. In this connection, physiology has gone about as far as it can go. But, with regard to the central problems of music, this is not the case: The science of music has still a long way to go.

For musical aesthetics, all this adds up to the view that those theorists who erect the principle of the beautiful in music upon the effects of feeling are lost, scientifically speaking. This is because they can know nothing about the nature of the relation between sensation and feeling, therefore, at best, they can only indulge in guesswork or fantasy. No artistic or scientific definition of music will ever be able to amount to anything if it is based upon feeling. No critic supports his estimate of the merit and significance of a symphony with a description of the subjective feelings by which he is overcome upon hearing it. Just as little can he, proceeding from the feelings, teach anything to musical aspirants. This latter point is important, because, if the connection of specific feelings with certain musical expressive devices were as well-founded as some people are inclined to believe (and as it must be if it is to keep the significance claimed for it), it would be an easy matter to lead budding composers almost to the highest degree of emotionally gripping effect. As a matter of fact, this has been attempted. In the third chapter of his *Der Vollkommene Kapellmeister,* Mattheson teaches us how pride, humility, and all passions are to be set to music. He tells, for example, that "inventions" intended to express jealousy must have "everything disagreeable, grim, and miserable."[24] Heinchen, another master of the preceding century, in his *Generalbaß*[25] gives eight sheets of examples of how music should express feelings of rage, cantankerousness, pomposity, timidity, or lovesickness.† So all it takes is to have such precepts as these begin with "Take a..." as in a cookbook or with "Rx..." as in a medical prescription. From such attempts, we get

---

*Du Bois-Reymond's address to the Congress of Natural Scientists in Leipzig "On the limits of our knowledge of nature" (1872) includes a new and valuable corroboration of this view.[23]

†The privy councillor and doctor of philosophy von Böcklin gives wonderful instructions on page 34 of his "Fragmente zur höherem Musik" (1811). Among others: "Suppose the composer wants to represent someone who has been insulted. In this music, aesthetical passions must come one after another, a sublime song leap out in sprightliest fashion, the inner voices rage, and shuddering tremolandos terrify the expectant listener."[26]

the very informative conviction that special rules of art are at once too narrow and too broad. There is no end to these rules for the musical arousing of specific feelings. They do not really belong to aesthetics, however, since the effect they seek is not purely aesthetical: An inextricable part of that effect is physical. The aesthetical recipe must show us how the musician produces beauty in music, not how he produces arbitrary effects in the audience. How altogether feeble these rules really are can best be shown by considering how magically potent they would have to be. For if the effect of each musical element were necessary and discoverable, we could play upon the feelings of the hearer as on a keyboard. And even if this were possible, would the purpose of art be thereby fulfilled? Precisely this is the legitimate question, and it answers itself in the negative. Musical beauty alone is the real strength of the musician. Upon its shoulders, he advances confidently through the stormy seas of time, in which the feelings offer him not even a straw to clutch.

We have now two questions, namely, what specific feature distinguishes the effects upon feeling caused by music, and whether this feature is essentially aesthetical. We can answer these questions through knowledge of one single factor: the powerful effect of music upon the nervous system. Upon this is based the characteristic intensity and immediacy with which music (by comparison with the nontonal arts) is capable of arousing feelings.

But the more powerfully an effect from a work of art overwhelms us physically (and hence is pathological), the more negligible is its aesthetical component. (Of course, this proposition cannot be inverted.) Regarding the making and the comprehension of music, another factor must be brought forward, which the purely aesthetical side of music represents and which, in contrast to the specifically musical stimulation of feelings, approximates the general conditions of beauty in all the arts. This is pure contemplation. In the next chapter, we shall examine the way it manifests itself outwardly in music, and the many-sided relationships it brings[27] to the life of feeling by means of music.

V

MUSICAL PERCEPTION:
AESTHETIC VERSUS
PATHOLOGICAL

Nothing has held back the development of musical aesthetics as noticeably as the excessive importance which some people have ascribed to the effects of music upon feeling. The more striking these effects were, the more highly they were extolled as harbingers of musical beauty. We, on the contrary, have seen that, on the hearer's part, a very powerful constituent of physical stimulation was mingled with precisely the most overwhelming impressions of music. On music's part, this intense urgency is situated in the nervous system not so much in its artistic moment, which after all comes from mind and addresses itself to mind, as in its material moment, which nature has endowed with that unfathomable physiological affinity. It is the elemental in music, i.e., sound and motion, which shackles the defenceless feelings of so many music lovers in chains which they rattle quite merrily. Far be it from us to want to underestimate the authority of feeling over music. But this feeling, which in fact to a greater or less degree unites itself with pure contemplation, can only be regarded as artistic when it remains aware of its aesthetic origin, i.e., the pleasure in just this one particular beauty.[1]

If this awareness is lacking, if there is no free contemplation of the specifically musical beauty, and if feeling thinks of itself as only involved in the natural power of tones, then, the more vigorously the impression makes its appearance, all the less can art ascribe such impression to itself. The number of people who hear music (or, strictly speaking, *feel* it) in this fashion is very considerable. While they in passive receptivity allow the elemental in music to work upon them, they subside into a fuzzy state of supersensuously sensuous agitation determined only by the general character of the piece. Their attitude toward the music is not contemplative but pathological. It is a constant twilight state of sensation and reverie, a drooping and yearning in resounding emptiness. If we play a few similar pieces, perhaps of a noisy, cheerful character, for an adherent of the feeling-theory, he will remain under the spell of the same impressions. Only what these pieces have in common, the effect of noisy cheerfulness, penetrates his awareness, while that which is special in every composition, namely, its artistic individuality, escapes him. The musical listener will proceed in precisely the opposite manner. The characteristic artistic construction of a composition, which in effect marks it off from a dozen similar compositions as a self-subsistent artwork, so dominantly occupies his attention that he considers its similar or dissimilar impressions upon the feelings to be of trifling significance. The isolated perception of an abstract feeling-content instead of the concrete artistic phenomenon is entirely characteristic of such musical cultivation as the feeling-theorist's. By analogy, if a landscape were suffused with an unusual light, only the intensity of it would appear to him; he would be entirely incapable of giving an account of the landscape itself. An unmotivated and therefore all the more forcible overall impression will be absorbed lock, stock, and barrel.*

Slouched dozing in their chairs, these enthusiasts[2] allow themselves to brood and sway in response to the vibrations of tones, instead of contemplating tones attentively. How the music swells louder and louder and dies away, how it jubilates or trembles, they transform into a nondescript state of awareness which they naively consider to be purely intellectual. These people make up the most "appreciative" audience and the one most likely to bring music into disrepute. The aesthetical criterion of intellectual pleasure is lost to them; for all they would know, a fine cigar or a piquant delicacy or a warm bath produces the same effect as a symphony. Some sit there mindlessly at ease, others in extravagant rapture, but for all the principle is one and the same: pleasure in the elemental in music. Incidentally, for people who want the kind of effortless suppression of awareness they get from music, there is a wonderful recent discovery which far surpasses that art. We refer to ether and chloroform. Indeed these drugs produce a supremely pleasant intoxication, the whole organism pulsating with sweet dreams, without our

---

*The infatuated Duke in Shakespeare's *Twelfth Night* is a poetical personification of such musical hearing. He says:

> If music be the food of love, play on;
> . . . .
> O, it came o'er my ear like the sweet south,
> That breathes upon a bank of violets,
> Stealing and giving odour!

And later, in Act II, he exclaims:

> Give me some music . . .
> Methought it did relieve my passion much. . . .

resorting to the vulgarity of winebibbing, which is in itself not without musical effect.

According to this pathological type of view, musical achievements are to be included along with the products of nature which delight us but which do not make us think, do not make us aware of a conscious creative intelligence. We can dreamily inhale the sweet fragrance of the acacia even with our eyes closed. However, creations of the human spirit preclude this entirely if they are not to be degraded to the level of the sensuous pleasures of nature.

In no other art is this possible to such a degree as in music, whose sensuous aspect at least permits a nonintellectual pleasure. Indeed, the aforementioned dying away of music, while the products of the other arts endure, resembles (to use a dubious analogy) the act of consuming something. We can talk about guzzling an aria, but not a picture, a church, or a play. That is why the pleasures of no other art are available for such casual use. The best compositions can be played as background music and can help us digest the roast pheasant. Music is at once the most aggressive of the arts and the most forebearing. We cannot help hearing the most deplorable street organ in front of our house, but not even a Mendelssohn symphony can compel us to listen.

In every art, the naive audience takes pleasure in the merely sensuous aspect, while the ideal content is perceived only by the cultivated understanding. However, the reprehensible kind of musical hearing which we have been describing is surely not the same thing as this naive pleasure. This unartistic apprehension of a piece of music does not single out the *strictly* sensuous aspect, i.e., the rich variety of the succession of sounds in itself, but rather its abstract general impression, as mere feeling. From this the preeminence in music which the ideal content assumes with regard to the categories of form and content becomes apparent. Of course, people used to consider that a feeling wafting through a piece of music was the subject, the Idea, the intellectual content, and, on the other hand, the artistically created, well-defined tonal sequences were considered the mere form, the image, the sensuous garb of that supersensuous conception. However, precisely the "specifically musical" part is the creation of the artistic spirit, with which the contemplating spirit unites in complete understanding. The ideal content of the composition is in these concrete tonal structures, not in the vague general impression of an abstract feeling. The form (as tonal structure), as opposed to the feeling (as would-be content), is precisely the real content of the music, is the music itself, while the feeling produced can be called neither content nor form, but actual effect. In the same way, the supposed material, that-which-represents, is precisely that which is structured by mind, while what is allegedly that-which-is-represented, namely, the impression of feeling, inheres in the physical substratum of the tones and in large part conforms to physiological laws.

From the foregoing considerations we can readily arrive at a correct estimate of the so-called "moral effects" of music, which were praised with such zeal by the other authors as a splendid counterpart to the previously mentioned "physical effects." According to this view, music is not in the least to be enjoyed as a kind of beauty but is to be perceived as a crude natural force which emerges through unconscious activity and is thus directly opposed to everything aesthetical. Moreover, what this putative moral effect of music has in common with the generally accepted physical effect is entirely superficial.

The creditor who, when pressing for repayment, was so moved by the sound of his debtor's music that he forgave the whole debt* is activated in no other way than the sluggard who is all of a sudden prompted by a waltz tune to dance. The former is moved more by the intellectual elements, harmony and melody; the latter, by the sensuous rhythm. Neither proceeds out of free self-determination, however; neither is yielding to the promptings of spirit or of love for beauty, but both are stirred as a result of neural stimulation. Music loosens the feet or the heart as wine the tongue. Such conquests tell us only about the vulnerability of the vanquished. To undergo unmotivated, aimless, and casual emotional disturbances through a power that is not *en rapport* with our willing and thinking is unworthy of the human spirit. When people surrender themselves so completely to the elemental in an art that they are not in control of themselves, then it seems to us that this is not to the credit of that art and is still less to the credit of those people.

It is not at all the purpose of music that it should be enjoyed in such a way, for all that its strong affective component makes this possible. This is the issue in which the oldest accusation against music has its root: That it enervates us, makes us flabby, causes us to languish.[4] Where music is administered as a stimulant to unspecified emotions or as nourishment for the feelings in themselves, that accusation becomes all too true. Beethoven insisted that music should "strike fire in the soul."[5] Note carefully that word *should.* It is open to question, however, whether or not a fire produced and nourished by music might inhibit the development of a person's willpower and intelligence. In any event, this indictment of the influence of music seems to us preferable to excessive glorification. Just as the physical effects of music stand in direct relation to morbid irritation of the nervous system accommodating itself to them, so the moral influence of tones increases with coarseness of mind and character. The scantier the vestige of refinement, the more powerfully does such influence penetrate. As is well known, music exercises the strongest effect upon savages.

This does not deter our moralists. They begin, as though warming up, preferably with numerous examples, telling how "even the animals" yield to

*As told about the Neapolitan singer Palma and others in A. Burgh, Anecdotes on Music, 1814.[3]

the power of music. And it is true: The call of the trumpet fills the horse with courage and eagerness for battle; the fiddle inspires the bear to attempt ballet steps; the delicate spider and the ponderous elephant are set in motion by hearing the beloved sounds.[6] But is it really so commendable to be a music lover in such company?

After the animals have performed their numbers, the old human chestnuts come onstage, mostly in the manner of the story about Alexander the Great, who, having been put into a rage by the flute-playing of Timotheus, was pacified by singing.[7] Similarly, the less famous King of Denmark, Eric the Good, in order to convince himself of the highly praised power of music, got a famous musician to play for him, having first ordered all weapons to be taken away. By his choice of modulations, the musician first moved all hearers to gloom, then to joy. Finally he raised a storm of frenzy. "The King broke through the door, grabbed a sword, and slew four bystanders." (Albert Krantzius, Dan. lib. V., cap. 3.)[8] And that, indeed, was the "good" Eric!

Were such "moral effects" of music still on the agenda, it is unlikely that anybody would rise indignantly to speak for or against the bewitching power which, in sovereign extraterritoriality, conquers and befuddles the human spirit with no regard for its thoughts and decisions. Yet the consideration that the most famous of these musical trophies belong to hoary antiquity makes it feasible to derive an historical perspective from all this. There can be no doubt at all that, for the ancients, music had a much more immediate effect than it has now, since humankind only just in its primitive stage of development is much closer to and more at the mercy of the elemental than later, when consciousness and self-determination come into their own. To this natural susceptibility, the particular condition of music in Greek antiquity accommodated itself to advantage. It was not art in our sense of the word. Sound and rhythm operated independently in almost total isolation, sketchily prefiguring the rich forms shaped by spirit which constitute the music of the present. Everything that is known of the music of that time points with certainty to the conclusion that it was merely sensuous but, on the other hand, was becoming increasingly refined, within its limitations. In classical antiquity, there was no music in the modern, artistic sense; otherwise it would have lost as little for later development as have classical poetry, sculpture, and architecture. (The predilection of the Greeks for exhaustive study of the subtlest tonal relationships, being pure science, does not belong in a work such as the present one.)

The lack of harmony, the confinement of melody within the narrowest limits of recitativelike expression, and finally the inability of the old system to evolve into an abundance of truly musical forms made impossible an unqualified acceptance of music as art in the strict sense. As well, it was almost never independent, being always used in connection with verse, dance, and mime, and hence as a complement to the other arts. Music's sole occupation was to animate by means of rhythmic pulsation and variety of tone-colour and ultimately as intensification of declamation, to comment upon words and feelings. Hence it was mainly with regard to its sensuous and symbolical aspects that music was effective. Under these confining circumstances, music was compelled to develop these aspects to greater, more subtle effectiveness. The refinement of melodic materials so far as the use of quarter tones and the "enharmonic genus" is just as little a product of our contemporary musical art as are the special expressive characteristics of the different tonalities and their close conformity to the spoken or sung word.

Moreover, these intensified relationships found for their narrow range a much greater responsiveness in the hearers. That the Greek ear was capable of grasping infinitely finer intervallic differences than ours is shown by equal temperament tuning. In the same way, the Greek disposition was far more open to and desirous of various mental alterations caused by music than we are, who cherish a contemplative kind of pleasure in the products of music art which paralyses music's elemental influence. So it stands to reason that the effects of music in antiquity should have been more potent.

A few of the historical narratives which have come down to us concern the specific effects of the different musical modes. They produce a basis for explanation, in the strict separation with which the individual modes were selected for specific purposes and were kept unmixed. The Greeks used the Dorian mode for solemn, especially religious occasions; with the Phrygian, they aroused the fighting passions of the army; the Lydian signified grief and melancholy; and the Aeolian resounded when they wanted to have a high old time with love or wine. Through this strict and deliberate separation of four principal modes for so many types of mental state, just as through their consequent association with poems which are compatible only with their own particular modes, the ear and mind must involuntarily acquire a marked tendency, upon hearing a piece of music, to reproduce promptly the feeling corresponding to its mode. Upon the basis of this lopsided development, music was then an indispensable, obedient accompaniment to all the arts, was a means to pedagogical, political, and other ends; it was everything but an independent art. If all it took to make soldiers fling themselves gallantly upon the enemy was a few flourishes in Phrygian and if the fidelity of grass widows could be assured by means of Doric songs, then the decline of the Greek modal system might be mourned by generals and husbands. But the aesthetician and the composer will squander no regrets upon it.[9]

According to our view, all such pathological ways of being affected by a piece of music are opposed to the deliberate pure contemplation of it. This contemplative hearing is the only artistic, true form; the raw emotion of savages and the gushing of the music enthusiast can be lumped together in a single category contrary to it. To the beautiful corresponds an enjoying, not an undergoing, as the term *aesthetic enjoyment* [*Kunstgenuß*] neatly signifies.[10] Of course the enthusiasts consider it a heresy against the omnipotence of music if a person denies the association with the revolutions and riots of the heart which they encounter in every piece of music and in which they sincerely participate. Obviously that person is "cold," "unfeeling," "cerebral." Nevertheless. It is a splendid and significant thing to follow the creative spirit as it magically opens up before us a new world of elements, coaxes them into all imaginable relationships with one another, and thus builds up, demolishes, produces, and destroys, controlling the entire wealth of a domain which elevates the ear into the subtlest and most highly developed of the sense organs. This is not a feigned emotion lacerating us with compassion. Joyfully, in unemotional yet heartfelt pleasure, we behold the artwork passing before us and realize better what Schelling so felicitously called "the sublime indifference of the beautiful."* Thus to take pleasure in one's own mental alertness is the worthiest, the wholesomest, and not the easiest manner of listening to music.

The most significant factor in the mental process which accompanies the comprehending of a musical work and makes it enjoyable will most frequently be overlooked. It is the mental satisfaction which the listener finds in continuously following and anticipating the composer's designs, here to be confirmed in his expectations, there to be agreeably led astray. It goes without saying that this mental streaming this way and that, this continual give and take, occurs unconsciously and at the speed of lightning. Only such music as brings about and rewards this mental pursuing, which could quite properly be called a musing [*Nachdenken*] of the imagination, will provide fully artistic satisfaction. Without mental activity, there can be no aesthetical pleasure whatever. But music is characteristically this type of mental activity par excellence, for the reason that its achievements are not static; they do not come into being all at once but spin themselves out sequentially before the hearer, hence they demand from him not an arbitrarily granted, lingering, and intermittent inspection, but an unflagging attendance [*Begleiten*] in keenest vigilance. This attendance can, in the case of intricate compositions, become intensified to the level of spiritual achievement. Like many individual persons, many whole nations are able to give over to it only with great difficulty. The tyranny of the upper vocal part among the Italians has one main cause in the mental indolence of those people, for whom the sustained penetration with which the northerner likes to follow an ingenious web of harmonic and contrapuntal activity is beyond reach. So the pleasure is more superficial for hearers whose mental activity is slight, and such musical tosspots are able to consume such quantities of music as make the artistic soul shudder.

---

*"Über das Verhältnis der bildenden Künste zur Natur."[11]

With every artistic pleasure, there is an indispensable intellectual aspect, as can be effectively demonstrated by the very different levels on which one and the same musical work can be listened to: With sensuous and sentimental people, the intellectual aspect can diminish to a minimum; with predominantly intellectual people, it becomes nothing short of crucial. The true "happy medium" [*recht Mitte*], in our view, here inclines preferably a bit to the right [*rechts*]. To become drunk requires only weakness, but true aesthetical hearing is an art.*

The person who wallows in feeling is in most instances untrained in the aesthetical comprehension of the musically beautiful. The layman is most likely to "feel" when he listens to music; the trained artist is least likely to do so. That is to say, the more prominent the aesthetical moment in the hearer (just as in the artwork), the more inconspicuous it makes the merely elemental. Hence the venerable axiom of the theoreticians, that melancholy music arouses feelings of sadness in us, and cheerful music, joyfulness, is to this extent not always correct. If every dull requiem, every noisy death march, every plaintive adagio had the power to make us sad, who would want to go on living? Let a composition [*Tondichtung*] gaze upon us with the clear eyes of beauty and we will fervently rejoice in it, however, even if it has all the grief of the century as its subject. But not always has the loudest jubilation of a Verdi finale or a quadrille by Musard made us cheerful.

The lay enthusiast likes to ask whether a piece of music is cheerful or sad; the musician, whether it is good or bad. These pithy maxims clearly show which of the two parties is in the right.

---

*It is altogether in keeping with W. Heinse's fanatical and dissolute character that he ignores the specifically musical beauty in favour of vague impressions of feeling. In his novel "Hildegard von Hohenthal," he goes so far as to say: "True music . . . everywhere sets out to communicate the feelings and the sense of the words so effortlessly and pleasantly to the listener that one does not notice the music. Such music endures forever; it is just so natural that one does not notice the music, but only the sense of the words comes across."

However, an aesthetical reception of the music, directly to the contrary, occurs only when the listener *notices* it entirely, when he listens to it attentively and is immediately aware of its beauties. Heinse, to whose own peculiar brand of naturalism we do not deny the tribute of admiration it deserves, is much overrated so far as poetry and (even more) music are concerned. On account of the scarcity of worthwhile writings about music, people have treated and quoted Heinse as if he were an eminent aesthetician. Can we, however, really overlook the way his writings, after a few striking aperçus, for the most part collapse into such a flood of platitudes and egregious errors that one is frankly alarmed at such lack of culture? Moreover, Heinse's warped aesthetical judgment, as revealed in his analyses of operas by Gluck, Jomelli, Traetta, and others (in which, instead of artistic instruction, we get almost nothing but enthusiastic proclamations), goes hand in hand with technical ignorance.[12]

When we said that our aesthetical pleasure in a piece of music was conditional upon its artistic merit, this did not mean that a simple horn call or a yodeller in the mountains could not occasionally evoke greater rapture in us than the most excellent symphony. In this instance, however, music joins the ranks of the *naturally* beautiful. Not as this particular tonal structure but as this particular type of natural effect, such sounds impinge upon the ear and, in keeping with the scenic surroundings and dependent upon our frame of mind, surpasses in influence every artistic pleasure. Here is a situation where the elemental can cause a more powerful impression than the artistic. Aesthetics, however, as the doctrine of the artistically beautiful, is supposed to account for music only on its artistic side and hence to recognize only those of its effects which music produces as a manifestation of the human spirit, through a particular construction brought forth in pure contemplation, out of those elemental factors.

The most indispensable requirement if we are to hear music aesthetically is, however, that we hear the piece *for its own sake,* whichever it be and with whatever comprehension we hear it. The instant music is put to use merely as a means to produce a certain mood in us or as an accessory or an ornament, it ceases to be effective as pure art. The elemental in music is forever being mistaken for artistic beauty itself, a part being taken for the whole, thereby giving rise to unutterable confusion. Many pronouncements about "the art of music" apply not to that art but to the sensuous effect of its physical materials. When the dying Henry IV of Shakespeare's play called for music, it was not with the intention of really listening to the performance, but for the purpose of letting it lull him into a dreaming state by means of its mere sound (*Henry IV Part II,* Act IV, Scene 4). Just as little would Portia and Bassanio in *The Merchant of Venice* have been disposed, in the fateful casket scene, to bestow attention upon the music. J. Strauss wrote charming, indeed brilliant music in his better waltzes, but it ceases to be so the moment we use it only to provide the beat for dancing. In all these instances, it is entirely a matter of indifference what piece it is, provided it has in a general way the required basic attributes. Only the person who retains not just the general aftereffects of feeling, but also the unforgettable, specific image of just this particular piece of music, has heard it and enjoyed it. Those edifying impressions upon our feeling and their profound psychological as well as physiological significance ought not to prevent a critique from rigorously separating the artistic from the elemental in any given effect. From an aesthetical point of view, music must be comprehended not so much as cause as effect, not as producer but as product.

Just as frequently as is its elemental effect, music's prevailingly harmonic nature, which is conveyed by measured repose and motion, dissonance and concordance, is confused with music itself. Considering the present situation of music and philosophy, in the interests of both, we should not go along with the ancient Greeks' extension of the notion of music to include all science and art and the cultivation of all the powers of the soul. The famous apology for music in *The Merchant of Venice* (Act V, Scene 1)* is based on such confusion of music itself with the dominating spirit of euphony, of agreement, of measurement. Generally speaking, we could without much alteration substitute "poetry," "art," or indeed "beauty" for "music" in such situations. That music is singled out from the ranks of the arts for special treatment is owing to the equivocal influence of its popularity. Elsewhere in that same speech from *The Merchant of Venice,* there is similar testimony to this, where the restraining effect of tones upon beasts is much extolled. Thus music turns up yet again in its role as animal tamer.

Bettina's "musical explosions" (as Goethe so gallantly called her letters on music)[13] provide the most instructive examples. The very prototype of all vague enthusiasm over music, Bettina shows how far one can overextend the notion of this art just to play about with it. With the pretension of speaking about music itself, she instead goes on about the obscure influence it has upon her feelings; she deliberately avoids giving any serious consideration to the luxuriant dreamlike bliss of this influence. For her a musical work is always an inscrutable product of nature, not a human artwork; hence she considers music to be nothing other than purely miraculous. Bettina calls "music" or "musical" any number of phenomena which merely have one factor or another in common with music: euphony, rhythm, arousal of feeling. It does not depend at all upon those factors, however, but upon the particular manner in which they appear in artistic creation as music. Of course, this music-besotted lady considers Goethe, and even Christ, great musicians, although of the latter nobody knows whether he was one or not; of the former, everyone knows that he was not.

We hold in high esteem the authority of historical cultivation and poetic freedom. We understand why Aristophanes in *Wasps* calls a cultivated person "wise and musical" ($\sigma o\phi \grave{o}v$ $\kappa a\grave{\imath}$ $\mu o\upsilon\sigma\iota\kappa\acute{o}v$),[14] and we find apt the remark of Graf Reinhardt concerning the "musical eyes" of Oehlenschläger.[15] Nevertheless scientific investigation should never ascribe to or presuppose of music any other concept than the aesthetical, unless we abandon all hope of ever establishing this tenuous science on a firm basis.

---

*   The man that has no music in himself,
     Nor is not moved with concord of sweet sounds,
     Is fit for treasons, stratagems and spoils. . . .

VI

THE RELATION OF
MUSIC TO NATURE

Every particular thing stands in some relationship to nature. This relationship is for each thing the most fundamental, most venerable, and most influential. Our understanding of this relationship is on the increase, as anyone knows who feels the pulse of our times, however casually. Throughout modern research runs a trend toward the natural aspect of all phenomena so strong that even the most abstract researches are gravitating toward the methods of the natural sciences. And aesthetics, if it is not to have just a mere semblance of life, must get to know both the gnarled root and also the delicate strand by which each of the particular arts is linked to its natural first principles. For musical aesthetics, the relation of music to nature opens the way to conclusions of the greatest significance. The arrangement of its most troublesome data and the solution of its most controversial problems hang upon the correct assessment of this relation.

The arts (considered for the present as *receiving from* nature and not yet as *reacting to* it) stand in a twofold relation to our natural surroundings: first, through the crude physical material out of which they create; second, through the beautiful content which they come upon for artistic treatment. In both, nature is related to the arts as a motherly dispenser of the first and most important dowry. In the interests of musical aesthetics, we must now examine this endowment and look into what wise nature (the more munificent for being wise) has done for music.

If one inquires into the extent to which nature provides material [*Stoff*] for music, it turns out that nature does this only in the most inferior sense of supplying the raw materials which mankind makes into tones. Mute ore from the mountains, wood from the forests, the skin and entrails of animals, these are all we find in nature with which to make the proper building materials of music, namely, pure tones. Thus initially we receive from mother nature only material for material; this latter is the pure, measurable tone, determined according to height and depth of pitch. It is the prime and indispensable requisite of all music. It forms itself into melody and harmony, which are the two principal factors of music. Neither is encountered in nature; they are creations of the human spirit.

Not even in the most rudimentary form do we perceive in nature the orderly succession of measurable tones which we call melody. Nature's successive auditory phenomena are lacking in intelligible proportion and evade reduction to our major and minor scales. But melody is the jumping-off point, the life, the original artistic manifestation of the realm of sound; all additional determinations, all inclusion of content, are tied to it.

Just as little as melody does nature (which itself is a marvellous harmony of all phenomena) know harmony in the musical sense, i.e., as the sounding together of well-defined tones. Has anyone ever heard a triad in nature? A chord of the sixth or seventh? Like melody, harmony (though in a much slower evolution) is a product of the human spirit.

The Greeks knew no harmony but sang at the octave or in unison, just as at present those Asiatic people do among whom singing is to be found. The use of dissonances (among which are the third and the sixth) developed gradually, beginning in the twelfth century, and until the fifteenth century music was restricted to modulations upon the octave. The intervals which now come under the rules of our harmony must have been acquired one by one and sometimes took a whole century for so modest an achievement. The most artistically advanced people of antiquity, just like the most learned composers of the early Middle Ages, did not know what our shepherdesses in the remotest Alps know: how to sing in thirds. It is not the case, however, that harmony came along and shed a whole new light on music; on the contrary, it has been there from the first day. "The whole tonal creation existed from that moment," said Nägeli.[1]

Accordingly, harmony and melody are not to be found in nature. Only a third element in music, this one being supported by the first two, existed prior and external to mankind: rhythm. In the gallop of the horse, the clatter of the mill, the song of blackbird and quail, a unity is displayed into which successive particles of time assemble themselves and construct a perceivable whole. Not all but many manifestations of nature are rhythmic. And of course supreme in nature is the law of duple rhythm: rise and fall, to and fro. What separates this natural rhythm from human music must be immediately evident. That is to say, in music there is no isolated rhythm as such, but only melody and harmony, which are manifested rhythmically. In nature, on the contrary, rhythm conveys neither melody nor harmony, but only incommensurable vibrations in the air. Rhythm, the sole musical element in nature, is also the first thus to be awakened in mankind, and the earliest to develop in children and animals. When the South Sea Islander bangs rhythmically with bits of metal and wooden staves and along with it sets up an unintelligible wailing, this is the natural kind of "music," yet it just is not *music*. But what we hear a Tyrolean peasant singing, into which seemingly no trace of art penetrates, is artistic music through and through. Of course, the peasant thinks that he is singing off the top of his head. For that to be possible, however, requires centuries of germination.

So we have considered the necessary basic ingredients of our music and have found that humankind did not learn from the natural surroundings how to make music. The history of music teaches how and in what sequence our present-day system developed; we have presupposed this. Here we need only keep in mind that melody and harmony have emerged slowly and gradually as creations of the human spirit, as have also our intervallic relationships and scales, the separation into major and minor according to the different placements of semitones, and finally the system of equal temperament, without which our western European music would not have been possible. Nature has endowed mankind only with the organs and the desire for singing and with the ability to construct a tonal system, bit by bit, upon the basis of the simplest relationships (the triad, the harmonic series). These alone will continue to be the changeless foundations of any further construction. One should be on guard against the error of thinking that this tonal system (our present one) necessarily exists in nature. That naturalists nowadays, as a matter of course, casually treat musical relationships as if they were natural forces in no way stamps the laws governing music as natural laws; this is a consequence of our endlessly expanding musical culture. Hand observed quite rightly that for this reason even our children, while still in the cradle, already sing better than mature savages. "If the diatonic scale existed in nature, every human would always sing in tune, and always perfectly."*

When we call our tonal system "artificial," we use this word not in the refined sense of something fabricated at will in a conventional manner. We mean it to designate merely something in the process of coming into being, in contrast to something already created by God. Hauptmann overlooks this when he calls the notion of an artificial tonal system "totally invalid," in that "musicians could just as little have determined the intervals and invented a tonal system, as linguists [*Sprachgelehrten*] could have invented the words and syntax of a language."† Language is an artifact in exactly the same sense as music, in that

---

*Hand, Ästh. d. T. I. 50. In the same place, Hand aptly adduces that the Gaels in Scotland share with the tribes of India the lack of the fourth and seventh, so their tonal sequence runs c, d, e, g, a, c. Among the physically well-developed Patagonians in South America, there is no trace of music or song.[2] Helmholtz recently in his *Lehre von den Tonempfindungen* has painstakingly set forth the evolution of our tonal system. His conclusions are entirely consistent with the above.

†M. Hauptmann, Die Natur der Harmonik und Metrik. 1853. S. 7.[3]

neither has its prototype in external nature, but both have come into being gradually, and both must be learned. Not linguists but nations built their language according to their character, incessantly improving and modifying it. Thus also our musicians ["*Tongelehrten*"] have not "constructed" music but have simply established and consolidated that which the prevailing, musically competent Spirit has, with rationality but not with necessity, unselfconsciously devised.* From this process, it follows that our tonal system also will undergo extension and alteration in the course of time. Yet so many and such significant developments are still possible within the prevailing laws of music that a basic change in the system seems a long way off. If, for example, the extension consisted in "the emancipation of the quarter tone," of which a contemporary writer would have it that there are indications in Chopin,† then theory, the teaching of composition, and musical aesthetics would change completely. So, for the time being, the musical theoretician cannot do much more about this prospect than merely acknowledge it as a possibility.

Against our claim that there is no music in nature, it will be objected that there is a wealth of diverse voices which wonderfully enliven nature. Must not the babbling of the brook, the slap of waves on the shore, the thunder of avalanches, the raging of the gale have been the incentive to and prototype of human music? Have all the murmuring, squealing, crashing noises had nothing to do with the character of our music? We must in fact reply in the negative. All these natural manifestations are nothing but noise, i.e., air vibrations of incommensurable frequencies. Seldom at best, and then only in isolated instances, does nature produce a tone, i.e., a sound of determinate, measurable pitch, high or low. Tones, however, are the basic conditions of all music. With whatever intensity or charm these musiclike manifestations of sound might stimulate us, they are not on their way to becoming human music; rather they are merely rudimentary intimations such as, to be sure, may often subsequently provide powerful stimuli to human music in its developed state. Even the purest phenomenon of the natural auditory realm, namely bird song, stands in no relation to human music, inasmuch as it cannot be accommodated to our scales. And the natural harmonics – which in any case are the unique and indisputable natural foundation upon which the more complex relationships of our music are founded – have been explained in their true significance. The natural harmonic series generates itself on the unison-tuned Aeolian harp, so it

---

*Our view is in agreement with the investigations of Jacob Grimm, who says: "Whoever has acquired the conviction that language was a spontaneous human invention will also be in no doubt concerning the source of poetry and music." (Ursprung der Sprache. 1852.)[4]

†Johanna Kinkel, Acht Briefe über Klavierunterricht. 1852, Cotta.[5]

must be grounded in natural law. Nowhere in nature is this phenomenon to be heard, however. In the absence of a definite, measurable fundamental tone on an instrument, no sympathetic overtones in the harmonic series will be heard. So mankind must ask in order that nature may give a reply. The phenomenon of echo is even more easily accounted for.

It is remarkable how writers, even competent ones, cannot get rid of the notion of there being music in nature. Even Hand, from whom earlier we cited examples which showed his correct understanding of the character of natural auditory phenomena and their incommensurability with human music, has a whole chapter on the topic of music in nature.[6] In it he says that natural auditory phenomena must also, *in a manner of speaking* [*gewissermaßen*], be called music. Krüger likewise.* Where it is a question of principle, however, there can be no "in a manner of speaking." That of which we become aware in nature either is or is not music. The decisive factor can only be the commensurability of tones, but throughout his book Hand emphasizes "spiritual inspiration," "the expression of inner life, inner feeling," "the power of spontaneity through which an inner self is able to articulate itself externally." According to this principle, bird song must be called music and the mechanical music box must not. But precisely the opposite is the case.[8]

The "music" of nature and the musical art of mankind are two separate domains. The transition from the first to the second is by way of mathematics. This is an important assertion with many implications. Of course, one might not think it so important if we had systematized our musical tones by means of calculations used deliberately. On the contrary, however, it happened through instinctive application of latent measuring and reckoning of primitive representations of quantity and relation, the regularities of which were later established by science.

For the reason that in music everything must be commensurable, while in the sounds of nature nothing is so, these two realms of sound remain almost irreconcilable. Nature does not give us the artistic materials for a complete, ready-made tonal system but only the raw physical materials which *we* make subservient to music. Not the voices of animals but their entrails are important to us, and the animal to which music is most indebted is not the nightingale but the sheep.

This discussion, which has formed only a foundation (though an indispensable one) for our investigation of the conditions of the musically beautiful, brings us a step higher in the aesthetical domain.

The measurable tone and the tonal system are, first of all, *that by means of which* the composer creates, not *what* he creates. As wood and ore were only material for tone, so the tone is only material for music. And there is yet a third

---

*Beiträge für Leben und Wissenschaft der Tonkunst, S. 149 ff.[7]

and higher sense of *material:* the sense of the subject matter, the represented idea, the subject. *Whence* comes this material? From where does the content of a particular composition emerge, the subject which makes it an individual and differentiates it from other compositions?

Poetry, painting, and sculpture have their inexhaustible source of material all around us in nature. Wherever the artist looks among the beauties of nature, he finds himself stimulated by material appropriate for creating works of art.

In the visual arts, the contribution of nature is most evident. The painter could delineate no tree, no flower, if it were not exemplified in external nature, nor could the sculptor a statue, without knowing the human figure in reality and taking it as a pattern. The same applies to fictitious subject matters, fabrications. These can never be "fictitious" in the strict sense. Does the "ideal" landscape not exist in the rocks, trees, water, clouds, and audible things which are exemplified in nature? The painter cannot paint what he has not seen and observed in detail. Be his paintings landscape or genre, an historical painter fabricates. If a contemporary of ours paints a Huss or a Luther or an Egmont, he has not actually seen his subject, but, for each of its components, he must have taken the model meticulously from nature: not this particular man but many men, how they move, stand, walk, how light falls on them, and how they cast shadows. The greatest reproach would be to call his figures "impossible" or "unnatural." The same applies to poetry, which has a much wider range of naturally beautiful prototypes. Men and their actions, feelings, and fortunes are material for the poem, the tragedy, or the novel, whether from our own observations or from tradition (since even tradition is among the materials encountered by the poet). The poet cannot describe a sunrise or a snowscape, portray an emotion, or put peasants, soldiers, misers, or lovers upon the stage, if he has not seen their prototypes in nature and so studied them or so peopled his imagination from tradition that they take the place of immediate observation.

If we now contrast these arts with music, we recognize that music nowhere finds a prototype, a material for its productions.

For music, there is no such thing as the beautiful in nature.

This distinction between music and the other arts (architecture alone resembles music in having no prototype in nature) is far-reaching and momentous.

A painter's or a poet's creative effort is a constant (imaginary or actual) tracing, copying; there is nothing in nature for music to copy. Nature knows no sonata, no overture, no rondo, but rather landscapes, genre scenes, idylls, tragedies. The Aristotelian thesis about the imitation of nature in art,[9] which was still current among philosophers of the preceding century, has been flogged to death and needs no further discussion here. Art should not slavishly imitate nature; it has to transform it. From this it is evident that, before there can be art, something has to be there to be transformed. This is precisely the prototype offered by nature, the naturally beautiful. The painter is moved to artistic representation by the occasion of encountering a delightful landscape, a group of people, a poem; the poet, by an historical event or a personal experience. But what is there in nature that a composer could point to and exclaim: "What a splendid prototype for an overture or a symphony!"? The composer cannot transform anything; he must create everything new. What the painter or poet encounters as a result of his contemplation of nature, the composer must elaborate out of his own introspection. He must wait for it, in its own good time, to sing and sound within him. He then becomes totally involved in it and creates from it something which has no counterpart in nature and hence none in the other arts, indeed none in this world.

It is not from any kind of partiality that, for painting and poetry, we included mankind among the beauties of nature, but, in the case of music, we withhold the artistic song that arises within the human breast. The singing shepherd is not an object of art but is already subject. So long as his song consists of measurable, orderly successions of tones, however simple, it is a product of the human spirit, whether devised by a shepherd boy or by Beethoven.

If, however, a composer makes use of actual national melodies, this is not natural beauty, since we must trace them back to someone who originated them. And anyway, from where did the originator get them? Did he find their prototypes in nature? This is the legitimate question, and the answer can only be negative. The folk song is not a found object, not a natural beauty, but the first grade of genuine art, that is to say, naive art. For music, it is no more a prototype created by nature than flowers and soldiers scribbled with charcoal in detention cells and other places are natural prototypes for painting. Both are man-made. For the graffiti, the originals in nature can be identified, but not for the folk song, because there is nothing to trace.

One falls into a frequently encountered confusion when one takes the concept of *material* in an extended and higher sense and points out that Beethoven indeed wrote an overture to *Egmont* or (lest the "to" emphasize the dramatic intention unduly) a piece of music called "Egmont"; Berlioz, a "King Lear"; Mendelssohn, a "Melusina." One asks: Have these narratives not supplied the composer with material just as they have the poet? Not at all. For the poet, these characters are genuine prototypes which he transforms; to the composer, they offer mere stimulus, indeed, poetic stimulus. For the composer, the natural beauty would have to be audible, just as for the painter it is visible and for the sculptor, tangible. The content of Beethoven's overture is not the character Egmont, not his actions, experiences, attitudes, but these are the content of the portrait "Egmont," of the drama *Egmont*. The contents of the overtures are sequences of tones which the composer has created entirely spontaneously, according to logical musical principles. For aesthetical contemplation, they are wholly autonomous and independent of the mental image of Egmont, with which only the poetical imagination of the composer has brought them into connection, no matter whether, in some inexplicable way, the image was suitable for initiating the invention of that sequence of tones or whether he invented the sequence of tones and then found the image of Egmont consistent with it. This connection is so loose and arbitrary that nobody hearing the music would have thought of its putative subject if the composer had not from the outset prompted our imagination through explicit designation of the piece. The splendid overture of Berlioz, in itself, has no more to do with the mental image we have of King Lear than has a Strauss waltz. We cannot emphasize this too strongly, since, concerning this, the most erroneous views are widely held. On the face of it, the Strauss waltz seems inconsistent with the image we have of King Lear, and the Berlioz overture seems, on the other hand, consistent with it, if we compare those two pieces with that image. For this comparison, however, there is no inherent reason other than an explicit constraint from the composer. We are compelled by a particular title to compare the piece with an object outside it and to evaluate the piece by an extramusical criterion.

Perhaps it could be claimed that Beethoven's "Prometheus" overture is not grandiose enough for its subject. We cannot come to this from the internal evidence of the music, however, nor can we demonstrate it by means of any musical gap or imperfection. It is perfect because it realizes its content completely; to realize its poetic theme analogously is a second, altogether different, undertaking. The poetic theme is contingent upon the title. Moreover, with regard to a musical work with a specific title, such a claim can only apply to certain specific qualities: that the music sounds sublime or pretty, sad or cheerful, or that it progresses from straightforward exposition to melancholy conclusion, etc. The material of poetry or painting imposes the requirement of a specific concrete individuality, not mere attributes. That is why it would be conceivable that Beethoven's "Egmont" overture could be titled "William Tell" or "Jeanne d'Arc." The drama *Egmont* and the portrait "Egmont" admit, at worst, the confusion that the person represented is some other person in the same situation, but not that it is an entirely different situation.

We can see how closely the relation of music to natural beauty is connected to the whole question of its content.

There is another objection someone might bring forward from the musical literature to support the view that music is a natural beauty. There are cases where composers have not just derived poetic incentive from nature (as above) but have directly reproduced actual audible manifestations from it: the cockcrow in Haydn's *The Seasons;* cuckoo, nightingale, and quail songs in Spohr's *Consecration of Sound* and in Beethoven's *Pastoral Symphony.* When we hear this imitation, however, and in a musical work at that, the imitation would have in that work not musical but poetical significance. We would hear the cockcrow displayed not as beautiful music, nor as music at all, but only as

the mental impression associated with this natural phenomenon. "I have –
almost – seen Haydn's *The Creation,*" writes Jean Paul to Thieriot, following a
performance of that work.[10] Familiar captions remind us: "It is early morning,"
"Mild summer night," "Springtime." Apart from this merely descriptive intention,
no composer has ever been able to use natural sounds directly for genuine
musical purposes. Not all the natural sounds on earth put together can produce a musical theme, precisely because they are not music,* and it does
seem significant that music can make use of nature only when it dabbles in
painting.

*Two things must be kept distinct. One is the misconception, mentioned above, that
natural sounds can be directly and realistically carried over into the artwork. As O. Jahn
pertinently remarked, this can only be permitted in exceptional cases as humour.[11] The
other is the case where materials [*Elemente*], present in nature, being to some extent
musically effective because of their rhythmic or sonorous character, are taken over by
composers, not as something to be "imitated," but as something that lends itself to their
impulse to create musical motifs out of autonomous musical beauty, which with artistic
spontaneity they conceive and actualize. Strictly speaking, this is not what some people
call "tone-painting." Examples of these materials include the rush and murmur of water,
bird song, wind and weather, whizzing of arrows, whirring of spinning wheels, etc. "The
poet makes use of this in speech as in rhythm, but in music it reaches much further,
since the musical elements are widely distributed throughout the whole of nature."
Wonderful examples exist in abundance from the classical masters, no less than from
our modern composers; in this respect, the latter are incomparably more refined than
the former.

VII

"CONTENT" AND "FORM"
IN MUSIC

Has music a content?

Since people first gave thought to music, this has been the question most passionately debated. It has been answered categorically in both the affirmative and the negative. Eminent people, mostly philosophers, have affirmed the contentlessness of music: Rousseau, Kant, Hegel, Herbart,* Kahlert, etc.[2] Of the numerous physiologists who support this view, Lotze and Helmholtz[3] are the most important and for us are noteworthy for their musical cultivation. Much the more numerous faction is on the other side in the debate, arguing for the content of music. These are the real musicians among writers, and the majority of people are of the same general conviction.

It seems a little odd that precisely those who are conversant with the technical principles of music are least able to break away from the error of a view which contradicts those principles, for which failure one might more readily excuse the abstract philosophers. This is because, on this point, many musical writers are more concerned with doing what they consider honour to music than they are with truth. They attack the doctrine of the contentlessness of music, not as one opinion against another, but as heresy against the articles of faith. The rival view seems to them a shameful misconception, crude blasphemous materialism: "What? The art which exalts and inspires us, to which so many noble souls dedicate their lives, the art which can serve our sublimest ideas – should it be burdened with the anathema of contentlessness? Is it a mere clockwork chime of the senses, mere empty tinkling?" With that kind of vociferation, which they usually let off with both barrels, although one

*Robert Zimmermann has most recently, in his *Allgemeine Aesthetik als Formwissenschaft* (Vienna, 1865), on the basis of Herbart's philosophy, rigorously worked out the formal principle for all the arts, including music.[1]

part of it has nothing to do with the other,[4] nothing can be either disproved nor proved. This is not a point of honour, not a token of sectarianism, but simply a matter of knowledge of truth. To arrive at this we must, above all, be clear about the concept under dispute.

It is the mixing up of the concepts of content [*Inhalt*], subject [*Gegenstand*], and material [*Stoff*] which has in this connection caused and still causes so much unclarity, since each uses for its own concept a different term or attaches different ideas to the same word. *Content* in its original and proper sense means what a thing holds, what it includes within itself. In this sense, the tones out of which a piece of music is made, which as its parts constitute it as a whole, are the content itself. Nobody is willing to accept this answer, dismissing it out of hand as something altogether self-evidently wrong, because we usually confuse *content* with *subject*. When we raise the question of the content of music, we have in mind the idea of subject (subject matter), which, as the ideal conception of the work, stands directly opposed to the tones as its material ingredients. In this sense of *material*, however, as the subject matter or topic dealt with in the work, music in fact has no material. Quite rightly, Kahlert vigorously argues that verbal descriptions of music should not be provided, as is not the case with painting (Ästh. 380), although he is wrong where he goes on to say that such verbal descriptions might in some cases provide "a remedy for failure to achieve aesthetic pleasure."[5] But it can clarify our question, which is: What is the content of music? If music actually had a content in this sense, i.e., a subject, the question about the "what" of a composition would necessarily have to be answered in words. An "indefinite content," which everyone can have a different opinion about and which everyone can only feel but not reproduce in words, is not at all a content in the present sense.

Music consists of tonal sequences, tonal forms; these have no other content than themselves. They remind us once again of architecture and dancing, which likewise bring us beautiful relationships without content. However each person may evaluate and name the effect of a piece of music according to its individuality, its content is nothing but the audible tonal forms; since music speaks not merely by means of tones, it speaks only tones.

Krüger, who is by far the best-informed proponent of musical "content" against Hegel and Kahlert, maintains that music merely presents another side of the same content which belongs to the other arts, painting, for example. "Every plastic form," he says (Beiträge, 131), "is static. It allows not action, but rather past action or the essence of action. Thus the painting does not tell us that this is Apollo conquering; rather it shows the conquerer, the enraged combatant," etc. He says that music, on the contrary, "gives the verb to that motionless plastic substantive, the activity, the inner surge. If, in the case of painting, we have recognized as true motionless content such attributes as 'enraged' or 'amorous,' then no less should we recognize, in the case of a piece of music, the true dynamic content: [Someone or something] rages, loves, rushes, surges, storms." This latter is only half true. Music can rush, surge, and storm, but it cannot love and be angry. These are inwardly felt passions. We here refer the reader back to our second chapter. Krüger continues by comparing the definiteness of painted content with the content of music. He says: "The visual artist represents Orestes pursued by Furies, as is made evident by the externals of Orestes' body: In eye, mouth, brow, and posture is the expression of flight, melancholy, despair; close to him are the shapes of the accursed Furies, who have him in their power in sovereign, dreadful grandeur, likewise externally visible in fixed outlines, features, postures. The composer represents Orestes being pursued, not in static outline, but from the point of view opposite to that of the visual artist: He sings of the horrors and trembling of his soul, of the impulse to struggle and flee," etc.[6] In my view, this is entirely false. The musician cannot represent Orestes in the one way or the other; indeed, he cannot represent Orestes at all.

It is not a valid objection that the visual arts are likewise unable to present to us the particular historical personage and that, unless we brought to it our knowledge of the actual historical situation, we would not be able to identify the painted shape as the individual. Certainly the painting is not Orestes, the man with these experiences and these biographical particulars; only the poet can represent these, because only the poet can narrate. Nevertheless, the picture "Orestes" unmistakably shows us a youth of aristocratic features, in Greek attire, with fear and mental anguish in his countenance and bearing; it shows us the hideous shapes of the goddesses of vengeance pursuing and tormenting him. What, in music, compares in definiteness with that visible (abstracted from the historical) content of the painting? Diminished sevenths, themes in the minor, tremolando bass, and the like: in short, musical forms which could equally signify a woman instead of a young man, pursued by bailiffs instead of Furies; jealous, vengeful, tortured by physical pain – anything imaginable, if we will grant that the piece signifies anything.

We have already established that, if we are to discuss the content and the representational capacity of music, we must base our discussion only on instrumental music. Surely nobody will so far forget this as to suggest that Orestes in Gluck's *Iphigenia* is a counterexample to the above. This Orestes comes not from the composer but from the poet's words, the actor's figure and mimicry, the designer's costumes and staging: These produce the complete representation. What the composer contributes is perhaps the most beautiful thing of all, but it is the very thing that has nothing to do with the creating of the actual Orestes: song.

Lessing has explained with wonderful clarity what the poet and the visual artist make out of the story of Laocoön. The poet presents by means of language the historical, individually distinct person Laocoön, whereas the painter and sculptor present an old man with two boys (of particular age, appearance, costume, etc.) crushed by the fearful coils of the serpent, the death agony shown in facial expression, attitude, and gesture. Lessing says nothing about the musician, as well he might not, since the musician can make precisely nothing out of the Laocoön story.[7]

We have already indicated how closely the question of the content of music is related to its situation with regard to natural beauty. The musician encounters no such prototype for his art as assures the other arts of the definiteness and recognizability of their content. An art which lacks prototypal natural beauty has, strictly speaking, no external shape. The original of its form of manifestation is nowhere to be found, hence we can have no concept of it. This art (i.e., music) reiterates no subject matter already known and given a name; therefore it has no nameable content for our thinking in definite concepts.

When we talk about the content of a work of art, we can really only make sense if we attach a form to it. The concepts of content and form mutually determine and complement each other. Where in thought a form does not seem separable from a content, there exists in fact no independent content. But in music we see content and form, material and configuration, image and idea, fused in an obscure, inseparable unity. This peculiarity of music, that it possesses form and content inseparably, opposes it absolutely to the literary and visual arts, which can represent the aforementioned thoughts and events in a variety of forms. Out of the story of William Tell, Florian made an historical novel, Schiller a drama, and Goethe began working on it as an epic. In all these cases, the content is the same; the difference is in the prose. Aphrodite rising out of the ocean is the identical content of innumerable painted and carved artworks, which are not confused with one another because of their form. In music there is no content as opposed to form, because music has no form other than the content. Let us consider this more closely.

The independent, aesthetically not further reducible unit of musical thought in every composition is the theme. The ultimate determinations which one ascribes to music as such must always be manifest in the theme, the musical microcosm. Listen to any principle theme you like, say, that of Beethoven's Symphony in B major. What is its content? Its form? Where does the one end and the other begin? We hope we have made it clear that no specific feeling is the content of the movement and that this will be no less apparent in the present concrete example. So what shall we say is the content? The tones themselves? Of course. But they are already formed. What shall we say is the form? Again, the tones themselves, but they are forms already fulfilled.

Every attempt in practice to separate form from content in a theme leads to contradiction or caprice. For example, if we repeat a theme on another kind of instrument or at a higher octave, does this alter the theme's content or its form? If, as usually happens, we say the latter, all that remains as content of the theme is the series of intervals as such, as the layout of notation in the score as it presents itself to the eye. But this is not a musical determination but an abstraction. It is like looking at the same view through windows with panes of many colours. The view is red, blue, yellow, etc. This, however, changes neither the content nor the form of the view, only the colour. Such innumerable changes of colour of the same forms, from the most dazzling contrast to the most delicate nuances, are entirely characteristic of music. And they constitute one of the richest and most highly developed aspects of its effectiveness.

A melody originally sketched for piano, which someone then orchestrates, acquires thereby a new form, but not form for the first time: It is already a formed conception. Still less would one want to assert that a theme changes its content through transposition and retains its form, since this view is doubly contradictory: The hearer would at one and the same time have to say that he recognizes the content as similar, but it sounds different.

Of course, in the case of whole compositions, particularly extended ones, we are accustomed to speaking of their form and content. This is not the original, logical sense of these concepts, but a particularly musical signification. By the "form" of a symphony, overture, sonata, aria, chorus, etc., we mean the architectonic of the combined components and groups of notes out of which the piece is made. Hence, more precisely, we mean the symmetry of these parts in their sequence, contrast, repetition, and development, in which case we understand the content to be the themes worked up into such an architectonic. Therefore there can be here no more question of a content as "subject," but solely of a *musical* content. Hence, in connection with complete musical works, the words *content* and *form* are used not in the purely logical, but in an artistic sense. If we want to subsume these concepts under the concept of music, we must proceed not with the complete (and therefore fully assembled) artwork, but with its ultimate, aesthetically not further reducible, nucleus. This is the theme or themes. In these, form and content in no sense suffer themselves to be separated. If we want to specify the "content" of a theme [*Motiv*] for someone, we will have to play for him the theme itself. Thus the content of a musical work can be grasped only musically, never graphically: i.e., as that which is actually sounding in each piece. Since the composition follows formal laws of beauty, it does not improvise itself in haphazard ramblings but develops itself in organically distinct gradations, like sumptuous blossoming from a bud.

This bud is the principle theme, the actual material and content (in the sense of subject matter) of the whole tonal structure. Everything in the structure is a spontaneous continuation and consequence of the theme, conditioned and shaped by it, controlled and fulfilled by it. It is as if it were a logical axiom, the rightness of which we take in at a glance, but which needs to be challenged and expounded by our intelligence in order for us to see what happens in the musical development of it, analogously to a logical demonstration. The composer puts the theme, like the principal character in a novel, into different situations and surroundings, in varying occurrences and moods – these and all the rest, no matter how sharply contrasted, are thought and shaped with reference to it.

Accordingly, we will perhaps call "contentless" that most spontaneous kind of preludising in which the player, relaxing more than working, launches forth into chords, arpeggios, and rosalias, without allowing an autonomous tonal configuration to come distinctly to the fore. Such free preludes are neither recognizable nor distinguishable as individuals; we might say that they have (in the wider sense) no content because they have no theme. The theme or, rather, the themes of a piece of music are therefore its essential content.

For a long time in aesthetics and criticism, due significance has not been given to the principle themes of compositions. After all, however, the theme reveals the mind which produced the whole work. When a Beethoven begins the "Leonore" overture or a Mendelssohn, his "Fingal's Cave," then every musician, without hearing another note of the piece, must recognize which palace he stands before;[8] but when we are confronted by the sounds of a theme like that of Donizetti's "Fausta" overture or Verdi's "Louise Miller," we need penetrate no further into the work to know that we are in the neighborhood pub. In Germany, both theory and practice put a disproportionate value upon the musical development of a theme, as opposed to *thematic substance*.[9] But whatever does not (explicitly or implicitly) lie ready in the theme cannot later be organically developed. And it is perhaps attributable less to lack of skill in thematic development than to lack of symphonic efficacy and fecundity of themes that our time has produced no more Beethovenian works.

Regarding the question of the *content* of music, we must take particular care not to use the word in its laudatory sense. From the fact that music has no content in the sense of "subject matter," it does not follow that music lacks *substance*. Clearly "spiritual substance" is what those people have in mind who fight with sectarian ardour for the "content" of music. (We must here refer to our third chapter.) Music is play [*Spiel*] but not frivolity [*Spielerei*]. Thoughts and feelings run like blood in the arteries of the harmonious body of beautiful sounds. They are not that body; they are not perceivable, but they animate it. The composer composes and thinks. He composes and thinks, however, at a remove from all objective reality, in tones. This is obvious, but it must be expressly repeated here, because it is all too often denied and violated by the very people who acknowledge it in principle. They think that composing is the translating of some kind of conceptual content into tones. But the tones themselves are the untranslatable, ultimate language. Indeed, from the very fact that the composer is forced to think in tones, it follows that music has no content, while every conceptual content must be capable of being thought in words. Although we have, in our investigation of *content*, had to exclude all music composed to specified texts as contradictory to the pure concept of music, yet the masterworks of the vocal repertoire are absolutely necessary for the assessment of the *substance* of music. From simple song to the most elaborate opera and the time-honoured religious celebration with church music, music has never ceased to accompany and thus indirectly to exalt the most cherished and significant activities of the human spirit.

Along with our vindication of the notion of the ideal substance of music, a second result must be emphasized. The subjectless formal beauty of music does not preclude its productions from bearing the imprint of individuality. The manner of artistic treatment, like the invention of this or that particular theme, is in each case unique: It can never be dissolved into a higher unity, but remains an individual. Thus, a theme by Mozart or Beethoven stands on its own feet as firmly and unadulteratedly as a stanza by Goethe, a dictum of Lessing's, a statue by Thorwaldsen, or a painting by Overbeck. Autonomous musical concepts (i.e., themes) have the trustworthiness of a quotation and the vividness of a painting: They are individual, personal, everlasting.

For this reason, we cannot share Hegel's view regarding the substancelessness [*Gehaltlosigkeit*] of music. Yet it seems to us even more erroneous that he attributes to this art only the articulation of the "unindividualised inner self." Even from Hegel's musical standpoint, which disregards the essentially formative and objective activity of the composer, interpreting music as free renunciation of subjectivity, the "unindividualisedness" itself does not follow, since the subjectively producing mind shows itself as essentially individual.[10]

In Chapter 3, we have touched upon how individuality leaves its mark by means of the choice and treatment of different musical elements. Regarding the accusation of contentlessness [*Inhaltlosigkeit*], music has content, but musical content, which is a not inconsiderable spark of the divine flame, like the beauty of any other art. But only by firmly denying any other kind of "content" to music can we preserve music's substance. This is because from indefinite feelings, to which at best such a content is attributable, no spiritual content derives; rather, in each composition, the content derives from its particular tonal structure as the spontaneous creation of mind out of material compatible with mind [i.e., the tones].

APPENDIX A

HERBART

(In the 6th edition (1881) of Vom Musikalisch-Schönen, *at the end of the first chapter, Hanslick inserted a quotation from J. F. Herbart, along with his own comment. This remained in all subsequent editions. Because it interrupts Hanslick's argument, I have placed it at the back as an appendix.* Translator.)

So far as I know, the first person to have attacked the feeling-theory in musical aesthetics is Herbart (in the ninth chapter of his Encyklopädie). Having declared himself opposed to the "interpretation" of artworks, he says:

> Fortune-tellers and astrologers have for millenia refused to allow it to be said that a person dreams because he sleeps and that the stars make their appearances now here and now there because they are in motion. In such manner, good connoisseurs of music reiterate the proposition that music expresses feelings. It is as if the feelings which (as it happens) are aroused by music and to the expression of which music (if you will) permits itself to be used lay the foundation of the general rules of simple and double counterpoint upon which their true essence is based. What might the old artists who developed the potential forms of the fugue . . . have intended to express? They did not want to *ex*-press [aus-*drücken*] at all. Their thoughts went not outward, but inward to the essence of art; but those who devoted themselves to "meanings" reveal their timidity in the presence of the inner self, and their partiality for outward display.*

Unfortunately, Herbart has not supported this opportune minority report in any detail and, along with these brilliant remarks, has written many foolish ones about music. In any case, however, his words as we have quoted them have not met with the attention they deserve.

---

*J. F. Herbart, *Kurze Encyklopädie der Philosophie* (Halle, 1831, pp. 124-25; *Werke*, 19 vols. (Langensalza, 1897), vol. 9, pp. 109-110.

APPENDIX B

SOME FEELING-THEORISTS

(At the end of the first chapter of Vom Musikalisch-Schönen, *in all editions, is a rogues' gallery of quotations from writers who upheld the "feeling-theory" of music. In Hanslick's nine revisions of the book, this section was relatively untouched except for the addition of Arrey von Dommer in the 3rd edition (1865) and of Richard Wagner in the 6th (1881). Hanslick's indifference to the proprieties of quoting and citing is nowhere more evident than here. I have ignored his minor alterations in the passages he quotes, such as words deleted and inversions of word order. But so many passages required detailed correction or amplification, alongside the quotation itself, that it seemed advisable to move the whole thing to the back as an appendix. That this section was an afterthought is evident from Hanslick's introductory note to it. This note follows.* Translator.*)*

Note. It seems to us hardly necessary for present purposes to attach the names of their authors to the views which we are here concerned to oppose, since these views are less the flowering of special convictions than the expression of a way of thinking which is generally becoming traditional. It is only in order to grant an insight into the widespread domination of these tenets that a few quotations from older and newer writers on music, out of the multitude available, are given space here.

MATTHESON: "We must as our main purpose with each melody produce a state of feeling in ourselves (if not more than one)." (Vollkomm. Kapellmeister. S.143.)

Johann Mattheson, Der Vollkommene Kapellmeister *(Hamburg, 1739; reprint ed. Kassel & Basel: Bärenreiter, 1954), p. 145. Hanslick has the page wrong.*

NEIDHARDT: "The ultimate purpose of music (the claims of the finest orators notwithstanding) is to arouse all feelings by means of tones and their rhythms alone." (Vorrede zur "Temperatur.")

J. G. Neidhardt, Beste und Leichteste Temperatur des Monochordi, etc. (Jena, 1706), p. 3.

J. N. FORKEL considers "figures" in music to be "the same as 'figures' (metaphors) in poetry and rhetoric, namely the expression of the different ways in which feelings and passions manifest themselves." (Über die Theorie der Musik. Göttingen 1777. S.26.)

J. N. Forkel, Ueber die Theorie der Music, insofern sie Liebhabern und Kennern nothwendig und nützlich ist (Göttingen, 1777), p. 26.

J. MOSEL defines music as "the art of expressing specific feelings by means of regulated sounds."

J. F. Mosel, Versuch einer Aesthetik des dramatischen Tonsatzes (Vienna, 1813). This work contains several passages from which the above may have been abstracted.

C. F. MICHAELIS: "Music is the art of expressing feelings by means of modulation of sounds. It is the language of emotion," etc. (Über den Geist der Tonkunst, 2. Versuch. 1800. S.29.)

C. F. Michaelis, Ueber den Geist der Tonkunst mit Rücksicht auf Kant's Kritik der ästhetischen Urtheilskraft, 2 vols. (Leipzig, 1800; reprint ed. Brussels: Culture et Civilisation, 1970), vol. 2, p. 29. Hanslick abbreviates considerably.

MARPURG: "The goal which the composer should set himself in his work is to imitate nature ... to arouse the passions at will ... to portray from life the emotions of the soul and the dispositions of the heart." (Krit. Musikus, 1.Band. 1750. 40.Stück.)

F. W. Marpurg, Des critischen Musicus an der Spree (Berlin, 1750; reprint ed. Hildesheim & New York: Olms, 1970), p. 323.

W. HEINSE: "The chief and ultimate purpose of music is the imitation, or rather the arousing, of the passions." (Musikal. Dialog. 1805. S.30.)

Wilhelm Heinse, Musikalische Dialogen, in Werke, 10 vols. (Leipzig: Insel, 1913), vol. 1, p. 217.

J. J. ENGEL: "A symphony, a sonata, etc. must embody the realization of a passion, which, however, resolves itself into multifarious sensations." (*Über musik. Malerei. 1780. S.29.*)

J.J. Engel, Ueber die musikalische Malerey (Berlin, 1780), p. 29. The above is less a translation than a paraphrase. Hanslick's vigorous pruning and Engel's archaic language make the "quotation" almost untranslatable.

Engel's words: "Eine Symphonie, eine Sonate, ein jedes von keiner redenden oder mimischen Kunst unterstüztes musikalisches Werk – sobald es mehr als bloß ein angenehmes Geräusch, ein liebliches Geschwirre von Tönen seyn soll – muß die Ausführung Einer Leidenschaft, die aber freylich in mannigfaltige Empfindungen ausbeugt, muß eine solche Reyhe von Empfindungen enthalten, wie sie sich von selbst in einer ganz in Leidenschaft versenkten, von aussen ungestörten in dem freyen Lauf ihrer Ideen ununterbrochenen Seele nach einander entwickeln" (pp. 29-30).

Hanslick's version: "Eine Sinfonie, eine Sonate u.s.w. muß die Ausführung einer Leidenschaft, die aber in mannigfaltige Empfindungen ausbeugt, enthalten."

J. Ph. Kirnberger: "A melodic phrase or theme [*Satz*] is an intelligible sentence [*Satz*], in the language of feeling, which allows a sensitive listener to feel the state of feeling which elicited it." (Kunst des reinen Satzes, II.Teil. S.152.)

J. P. Kirnberger, Die Kunst des reinen Satzes in der Musik, 2 vols. (Vienna, 1793).

Kirnberger's words: "Die Erfindung eines einzigen melodischen Satzes oder Einschnittes, der ein verständlicher Satz aus der Sprache der Empfindung ist, und einem empfindsamen Zuhörer die Gemühtslage, die ihn hervorgebracht hat, fühlen läßt, ist schlechterdings ein Werk des Genies und kann nicht durch Regeln gelehrt werden."

Hanslick's version: "Ein melodischer Satz (Thema) ist ein verstandlicher Satz aus der Sprache der Empfindung, der einen empfindsamen Zuhörer die Gemütslage, die ihn hervorgebracht hat, fühlen läßt."

Pierer's Universallexikon (2. Auflage): "Music is the art of representing feelings and mental states by means of beautiful sounds. It ranks higher than poetry, which is capable of representing only [!] such sentiments as are recognizable with the intellect, since music expresses wholly inexplicable feelings and ideas."

H. A. Pierer, Universal-Lexikon der Gegenwart und Vergangenheit, 3rd ed. (Altenburg, 1844), s.v. "Musik." (I have not had access to the 2nd edition cited by Hanslick.) Hanslick compresses slightly; the [!] is his.

G. SCHILLING'S Universallexikon der Tonkunst has the same interpretation under "Music."

G. Schilling, Encyclopädie der gesammten musikalischen Wissenschaften, etc. (Stuttgart, 1837; reprint ed. Hildesheim: Olms, 1974), s.v. "Musik."

KOCH defines music as "the art of expressing an agreeable play of sensations by means of sounds." (Musik. Lexikon: "Musik.")

H. C. Koch, Musikalisches Lexikon (Frankfurt, 1802), s.v. "Musik."
Koch's words: "Musik. Mit diesem aus dem Griechischen abstammenden Worte bezeichnet man heut zu Tage die Kunst durch Töne Empfindungen auszudrücken."
Hanslick's version: "Koch definiert die Musik als die 'Kunst, ein angenehmes Spiel der Empfindungen durch Töne auszudrücken'."

A. ANDRÉ: "Music is the art of producing tones which portray, arouse, and sustain sensations and passions." (Lehrbuch der Tonkunst I.)

A. André, Lehrbuch der Tonsetzkunst, 2 vols. (Offenbach, 1832), vol. 1, p. 1.
André's words: "Die Musik is die Wissenschaft und Kunst, durch Töne unsere Empfindungen auszudrücken."
Hanslick's version: "Musik ist die Kunst, Töne hervorzubringen, welche Empfindungen und Leidenschaften schildern, erregen und unterhalten."

SULZER: "Music is the art of expressing our passions by means of tones, as we do in speech by means of words." (Theorie der schönen Künste.)

J. G. Sulzer, Allgemeine Theorie der Schönen Künste, 2nd ed. (Leipzig, 1793; reprint ed. Hildesheim: Olms, 1967-70), s.vv. "Ausdruck," "Kunst," "Musik," et passim. Hanslick's "quotation" appears to be a composite abstract from these and other parts of Sulzer's four volumes.

J. W. BÖHM: "Harmonious sounds of strings engage not the understanding, not reason, but only the faculty of feeling." (Analyse des Schönen der Musik. Wien 1830. S.62)

J. W. Böhm, Analyse des Schönen der Musik (Vienna, 1830), p. 62.
Böhm's words: "... nicht den Verstand, nicht die Vernunft, sondern nur das Gefühlsvermögen beschäftigen der Seiten harmonische Töne...."
Hanslick gives "Seiten" as "Saiten." This seems, for once, a justifiable alteration.

GOTTFRIED WEBER: "Music is the art of expressing feelings by means of tones." Theorie der Tonsetzkunst, 2.Aufl. I.Bd. S.15.

G. Weber, Versuch einer geordneten Theorie der Tonsetzkunst, 3rd ed., 3 vols. (Mainz, Paris & Antwerp, 1830-32), vol. 1, p. 17. (I have not had access to the 2nd edition cited by Hanslick.)

Weber's words in the 3rd edition: "... sie ist die Kunst, Tonverbindungen, Tonstücke zu erfinden, welche Empfindungen, nach den Gesetzen der Schönheit ausdrücken...."

Hanslick's version: "Die Tonkunst ist die Kunst, durch Töne Empfindungen auszudrücken."

F. HAND. "Music represents feelings. Both in itself and hence also in music, every feeling and every mental state has its own particular sound and rhythm." (Aesthetik der Tonkunst, I. Band. 1837. §24.)

F. Hand, Aesthetik der Tonkunst, 2 vols. (Leipzig, 1837), vol. 1. The "quotation" is another of Hanslick's composites.

Hand's words in Chapter 2, §24: "[Die Musik] stellt Gefühle, aber nicht objective Gegenstände der Gefühle dar..." (p. 83).

Hanslick reduces this to: "Die Musik stellt Gefühle dar."

Hand's words in Chapter 2, §27: "Jedes Gefühl and jeder Gemütszustand hat an sich und so auch in der Musik seinen besondern Ton und Rhythmus..." (p. 88). This Hanslick quotes accurately.

In the first three editions of Vom Musikalisch-Schönon, *Hanslick "quoted" at greater length from Hand, including the above. In the 4th edition (1874), he reduced the segment to the two fragments given above, and so it has remained in all subsequent editions.*

AMADEUS AUTODIDAKTUS: "Music originates and takes root only in the spiritual world of feelings and sensations. Musically melodic tones [!] sound forth, not to the understanding, which, after all, only describes and analyzes... it speaks to feeling," etc. (Aphorismen über Musik. Leipzig 1847. S.329).

Amadeus Autodidactos (H.F.W. Richter), Aphorismen über Musik (Leipzig, 1847), p. 329.

Amadeus's words: "Die Tonkunst dagegen entquillt nur und wurzelt nur in der Welt der geistigen Gefühle und Empfindungen. Melodische musikalische Töne erklingen nicht dem Verstande, welcher Empfindungen beschreibt und zergliedert, sondern drücken solche aus und erregen solche auf mannigfach verschiedene Art und Weise, indem sie das menschliche Gemüth auf eine, in mancher Hinsicht noch unerklärbare Art und Weise durchströmen; kurz, musikalische Töne sprechen durch ihren Ausdruck zu dem Gemüth, nicht aber zu dem Verstand und der Einbildungskraft des Menschen, wie diess die Wortsprache thut."

Hanslick inserts a bit of ridicule: "Die Tonkunst entquillt und wurzelt nur in der Welt der geistigen Gefühle und Empfindungen. Musikalische melodische Töne [!] erklingen nicht dem Verstande, welcher Empfindungen ja nur beschreibt und zergliedert, ... sie sprechen zu dem Gemüt," etc.

FERMO BELLINI: "Musica è l'arte, che esprime i sentimenti a le passioni col mezzo di suoni." (Manuale di Musica. Milano, Ricordi. 1853.)

F. Bellini, Manuale della Musica (Milan, 1853), p. 2. Hanslick quotes accurately enough, but here is Bellini's actual sentence, along with the next two: "Moralmente, si definisce la musica come arte che esprime i sentimenti e le passioni col mezzo dei suoni. Fisicamente, qual Arte di combinare i suoni fra loro sotto certe forme e condizione. He pure la definizione di Arte o sistema di operationi, che ha il suono per oggetto e per elemento."

FRIEDRICH THIERSCH, Allgemeine Ästhetik (Berlin 1846) §18. S.101: "Music is the art of expressing or arousing feelings and mental states by means of the selection and combination of tones."

F. Thiersch, Allgemeine Aesthetik in akademischen Lehrvorträgen (Berlin, 1846), p. 101.

A. V. DOMMER: Elemente der Musik (Leipzig 1862): "Purpose of music: Music should arouse feelings in us and thereby produce mental images." (S.174.)

A. von Dommer, Elemente der Musik (Leipzig, 1862), p. 174. (The words "Purpose of music" belong to a marginal note.)

RICH. WAGNER, "Das Kunstwerk der Zukunft" (1850. Gesam. Schr. III, 99 und ähnlich sonst): "The voice of the heart is tone, and its artistically intentional speech is music [*Tonkunst*]." Of course, in the later writings, Wagner's definitions became even more nebulous; there music is for him just "Art of expression generally" (in "Oper und Drama," ges. Schriften III, 343), which to him seems to qualify as "the Idea of the World," "the essence of things grasped in its most immediate manifestation," etc. ("Beethoven," 1870, S.6 ff.)

Richard Wagner, Sämtliche Schriften und Dichtungen, 5th ed., 12 vols. (Leipzig: Breitkopf & Härtel, 1911). Quotation from Das Kunstwerk der Zukunft, vol. 3, p. 81; from Oper und Drama, vol. 3, pp. 274, 278 et passim; from "Beethoven," vol. 9, pp. 66 ff.

ESSAY: TOWARDS A
REVISED READING OF HANSLICK

The foregoing is a wholly new English translation of Eduard Hanslick's *Vom Musikalisch-Schönen,* not a revision of an existing one. The sole previous English translation, Gustav Cohen's *The Beautiful in Music,* first appeared in 1891.[1] I have undertaken to produce a successor to it because I have found that, in important respects, it fails to convey Hanslick's thought as embodied in the original German text.

In this Essay, I shall not parade my little triumphs over Cohen, specific points at which I may have come closer to the mark than he did, because it was not point-by-point that I translated the text, but as a continuous argument; the differences between Cohen's translation and mine are basic and pervasive. Instead I shall comment here on just two major differences between Cohen and myself: first, with regard to the title of the book; second, with regard to Hanslick's most famous statement of his main thesis, *"Der Inhalt der Musik sind tönend bewegte Formen."*

Titles beginning with "on the" or "concerning" (in German *von* or one of its modifications) are usually intended to convey in a nutshell what the book is about, and the present instance is no exception. So, if a translator gets the title wrong, we are entitled to doubt that he got much of the book right. Even more may we doubt this if he also mistranslates the most emphatic statement in the whole book of the main thesis of the book itself. Cohen erred on both counts, with the result that, from the sixth paragraph of Chapter 3 to the end of the book, he rarely makes contact with Hanslick's argument.

1. The title: "Vom Musikalisch-Schönen"

Gustav Cohen translates Hanslick's title *"Vom Musikalisch-Schönen"* with the words "The Beautiful in Music." As a translation of the somewhat eccentric German, this formulation is quite acceptable, provided one ignores the argument of the book. As the hyphen in the German original of the title indicates, Hanslick in his book uses the word *beautiful* [*das Schöne*] in a sense peculiar to music, while *the beautiful* in Cohen's rendering is used in a wider sense. Anyone looking at Cohen's words *The Beautiful in Music* would suppose that the translator is using the word *beautiful* in an abstract generic sense: There is a genus *the beautiful*, of which two species are *the beautiful in nature* (let us say) and *the beautiful in the fine arts;* in the fine arts, there are subspecies of *the beautiful*, such as *the beautiful in poetry, the beautiful in painting,* and *the beautiful in music*.

Anyone would have to suppose from Cohen's version of the title that Hanslick's book is about the last of these, *the beautiful in music,* but it is not. The book is about a special sense of *the beautiful* applicable only to music and not at all to the other arts. There may be a sense of *the beautiful* common to all the other arts or to all the arts including music, but Hanslick does not go into this. What he does go into – and very systematically – is a sense of the word *beautiful* which separates music from all the other arts, a separation which he explains in terms of form and content.

Music is unique among the arts, says Hanslick, in that its form *is* its content and (what amounts to the same thing) its content *is* its form; in the other arts, content and form are separable in significant respects, but not in the art of music. And, in music, the form that is content (or the content that is form) is precisely the *musically beautiful, das Musikalisch-Schöne,* and *this* is what Hanslick's book is about.

According to him, the beauty of a painting is, at least in part, dependent upon the beauty of its content (e.g., a beautiful flower girl or the conception of girlish innocence); the beauty of a poem is, at least in part, likewise dependent upon its content (e.g., an episode in the life of a hero or the conception of courage or of magnanimity); but the beauty of a musical artwork comes from nowhere outside itself and is therefore autonomous, self-subsistent.

There is nothing corresponding to the musically beautiful in any of the other arts, according to Hanslick. A translation of his title which does not plainly reflect the uniqueness of the musically beautiful is misleading and is evidence of something seriously wrong with the translator's understanding of the text itself.

It will have been noticed that the foregoing account of the musically beautiful in Hanslick's book is entirely negative, so it might be asked: In positive terms, what is this exclusive and self-subsistent beauty that is both form and content of music? The answer: *"tönend bewegte Formen"* (Hanslick); *"sound and motion"* (Cohen's rendering); *"tonally moving forms"* (mine).

2. *The positive main thesis: "Der Inhalt der Musik sind tönend bewegte Formen."*

At this point, we have to sidestep a small trap set by Hanslick. In his Foreword, for purely polemical reasons, he identifies as his main thesis in the book a certain negative thesis (to which we come in a moment), implying that its correlative positive proposition is in some sense minor and secondary to it. His whole argument, and the overall structure of the book, however, warrant our ignoring this priority and regarding the positive thesis (to which also we come in a moment) as actually the main thesis.

The "one main thesis, a negative one"[2] is not stated by Hanslick in the traditional form of a proposition; rather, it is scattered about in the Foreword, but it can be paraphrased thus: The defining purpose of music is *not* to represent (or express or arouse) feelings.[3] Here is Hanslick's positive thesis, as explicitly stated in the Foreword: "The beauty of a piece of music is specifically musical, i.e., is inherent in the *tonal relationships* [*Tonverbindungen*] without reference to an extraneous, extramusical context."[4] This quotation can be regarded as a preliminary version of the book's main thesis, as stated in our heading above. In it the words *tonal* and *relationships* are mutually explanatory: The relationships in question are exclusively *tonal,* and *tones* in the relevant sense exist only as related. I shall try to explain this sense.

In Chapter 6 of *Vom Musikalisch-Schönen,* Hanslick presents a definition which is of the utmost importance for this present discussion. He says that a *tone* [*Ton*] is "a sound of determinate, measurable pitch, high or low" [*ein Klang von bestimmter, meßbarer Höhe und Tiefe*] and that "tones . . . are the basic conditions of all music."[5]

Notice that, in Hanslick's definition, a tone is a specific kind of sound. In some contexts, *tone* is synonymous with *sound* in English, and *Ton* with *Klang* in German, but not in this context. Here tones are sounds of a particular kind, namely, of determinate, measurable pitch. *Determinate* [*bestimmt*] means possessing an identifiable character; *measurable* [*meßbar*] means standing in a certain relationship to something else. The *tonic* degree of a major or minor musical scale possesses the character of extreme stability or centrality; no other degree of a scale possesses this character to the same extent or in the same manner; each degree of the scale is different from every other in this regard. And each degree of the scale stands in a certain perceivable relationship to every other degree of the scale, a specific relationship of more or less tension, of attraction or repulsion.

In this sense, a "tone" is a sound, actual or imagined, perceived as occupying a position in a diatonic musical scale. The German word *Tonleiter* is wonderfully suggestive: a ladder whose rungs are tones. "The tones" collectively make up the whole diatonic system of music and are, as we shall see, the material out of which music is made, according to Hanslick.

Elsewhere[6] I have tried to show that this is familiar German usage with regard to the word *Ton* in discourse about music and music theory and that Hanslick's whole account of music in *Vom Musikalisch-Schönen* calls for this interpretation of *Ton*, plural *die Töne*, and many of the German words built upon the *ton-* prefix or root. Here I shall try to show that this is almost invariably the sense in which Hanslick uses the word in Chapter 3, which contains the central account of his positive doctrine regarding the nature of music, and that this doctrine cannot be rightly understood using the word in some other sense, as Cohen does. Almost invariably he translates it as *sound*. (All emphases are mine in the following quotations.)

EXAMPLE A

Hanslick asks: "What kind of beauty is the beauty of a musical composition [Ton*dichtung*]?" His reply:

> Es ist ein spezifisch Musikalisches. Darunter verstehen wir ein Schönes, das unabhängig und unbedürftig eines von außen her kommenden Inhalts, einzig in den *Tönen* und ihrer künstlerischen Verbindung liegt (page 72).

> *Cohen:* Its nature is specifically musical. By this we mean that the beautiful is not contingent upon nor in need of any subject introduced from without, but that consists wholly of *sounds* artistically combined (page 47).

> *Payzant:* It is a specifically musical kind of beauty. By this we understand a beauty that is self-contained and in no need of content from outside itself, that consists simply and solely of *tones* and their artistic combination (page 28).

The topic of this quotation is by now familiar: the nature of the specifically musically beautiful. The passage makes a tentative connection between the musically beautiful and the tones, a connection which subsequent examples will refine and elaborate. Here it will suffice to notice that *sounds*, as in Cohen's rendering, while not wrong, is too general: His sentence does not tell us much, while Hanslick's conveys something quite precise about music.

EXAMPLE B

Das Material, aus dem der *Ton*dichter schafft, und dessen Reichtum nicht verschwenderisch gedacht werden kann, sind die gesamten *Töne*, mit der in ihnen ruhenden Möglichkeit zu verschiedener Melodie, Harmonie und Rhythmisierung (page 73).

Cohen: The crude material which the composer has to fashion, the vast profusion of which it is impossible to estimate fully, is the entire *scale of musical notes* and their inherent adaptability to an endless variety of melodies, harmonies, and rhythms (page 47).

Payzant: The material out of which the composer creates, of which the abundance can never be exaggerated, is the entire system of *tones*, with their latent possibilities for melodic, harmonic, and rhythmic variety (page 28).

It is interesting here to observe how close Cohen came to recognizing that his customary *sounds* would not fit. Obviously what he means here by *musical notes* is what I mean by *tones*, except that his term lacks the precision the context requires.

A few lines further, Hanslick asks and answers:

Fragt es sich nun, was mit diesem *Ton*material ausgedrückt werden soll, so lautet die Antwort: Musikalische Ideen (page 73).

Cohen: To the question: What is to be expressed with all this material? the answer will be: Musical ideas (page 48).

Payzant: If now we ask what it is that should be expressed by means of this *tone*-material, the answer is: musical ideas (page 28).

EXAMPLE C

Die Formen, welche sich aus *Tönen* bilden, sind nicht leer, sondern erfüllte, nicht bloße Linienbegrenzung eines Vakuums, sondern sich von innen heraus gestaltender Geist (pages 78-79).

Cohen: The forms created by *sound* are not empty; not the envelope enclosing a vacuum, but a well, replete with the living creation of inventive genius (page 50).

Payzant: The forms which construct themselves out of *tones* are not empty but filled; they are not mere contours of a vacuum but mind giving shape to itself from within (page 30).

Cohen's rendering here, like many of his renderings, would be acceptable in isolation from Hanslick's text, indeed more acceptable than many of his. "Forms created by sound" is a partial definition of *tones* in Hanslick's sense, but missing from it is reference to the ideal and spontaneous character of the tones. The German original emphasizes these two characteristics; I have tried to preserve the spontaneity by retaining the reflexivity of *"sich bilden"*: "The forms which construct themselves out of tones...."An alternative is "The forms which build (or construct) out of tones..."; this would be perhaps more correct in isolation but would miss an important point Hanslick makes here and elsewhere regarding the tones.

EXAMPLE D

Jede Kunst hat zum Ziel, eine in der Phantasie des Künstlers lebendig gewordene Idee zur äußeren Erscheinung zu bringen. Dies Ideelle in der Musik ist ein *ton*liches, nicht ein begriffliches, welches erst in *Töne* zu übersetzen wäre (page 82).

Cohen: The object of every art is to clothe in some material form an idea which has originated in the artist's imagination. In music this idea is an *acoustic* one; it cannot be expressed in words and subsequently translated into *sounds* (page 52).

Payzant: Every art has as its goal to externalize an idea actively emerging in the artist's imagination. In the case of music, this idea is a *tonal* idea, not a conceptual idea which has first been translated into *tones* (pages 31-32).

This example emphasizes the ideal character of tones and of tonal structures.

EXAMPLE E

Wie aus dem gleichen Marmor der eine Bildhauer bezaubernde Formen, der andere eckiges Ungeschick heraushaut, so gestaltet sich die *Ton*leiter unter verschiedenen Händen zur Beethovenschen Ouverture oder zur Verdischen (page 92).

Cohen: As the same block of marble may be converted by one sculptor into the most exquisite forms, by another into a clumsy botch, so the *musical scale,* by different manipulation, becomes now an overture of Beethoven, and now one of Verdi (page 57).

Payzant: Just as out of the same marble one sculptor carves ravishing forms, the other clumsy botchings, so the *musical scale* in different hands takes on the form of a Beethoven overture or one by Verdi (page 35).

Here Cohen and I have the same problem: There is no equivalent in English to the German *Tonleiter.* I have included this example, however, not to reiterate this point but in order to present the sequel. Hanslick asks: "What makes the difference between these two compositions? That the one represents a heightened emotion, perhaps, or the same emotion more faithfully?" His answer:

... daß sie schönere *Tonformen* bildet (page 92).

Cohen: ... its *musical structure* is more beautiful (page 57).

Payzant ... it is constructed in more beautiful *tone*-forms (page 35).

EXAMPLE F

(The subject of the following sentence is the imagination of the gifted composer.)

... sie wird *Ton*formen bilden, die aus freiester Wilkür erfunden und doch zugleich durch ein unsichtbar feines Band mit der Notwendigkeit verknüpft erscheinen (pages 93-94).

Cohen: He will call into being *forms of music* which seemingly are conceived at the composer's pure caprice and yet, for some mysterious and unaccountable reason, stand to each other in the relation of cause and effect (page 58).

Payzant: It will construct *tone-forms* which appear to be devised out of free choice yet are all necessarily linked together by an imperceptible, delicate thread (page 36).

Cohen's rendering of this passage is one of his most desperate and rhapsodic. It seems that he considered *Tonformen* to be such musical forms as canon, fugue, sonata, first movement, and the like. But this is not Hanslick's sense of the word *form,* as I hope will become clear. The passage clearly shows that the forms in question are products of the imagination of the composer.

I think I need not belabour the point further in this manner. There is, however, a rather long passage of considerable interest, which, I believe, will bring together the main points I have been trying to exhibit by means of the brief passages compared above between Hanslick, Cohen, and myself. I shall quote my own translation of the passage, inserting Hanslick's German and Cohen's English at appropriate points and interposing a few comments of my own. The passage begins at my page 30, Cohen's page 50, and Hanslick's page 79.

It is due to a kind of subconscious recognition that we speak of musical "thoughts," and, as in the case of speech, the trained judgment easily distinguishes between genuine thoughts and empty phrases. In the same way, we recognize the rational coherence of a *group of tones* and call it a sentence, ...

The words I have emphasized, "group of tones," translate Hanslick's word *Tongruppe*. Cohen ignores the word.

The gratifying reasonableness which can be found in musical structures is based upon certain fundamental laws of nature governing both the human organism and *the external manifestations of sound* [die äußeren Lauterscheinungen; Cohen: *"the phenomena of sound"*]. It is mainly the law of harmonic progression ... which produces the nucleus of the most significant musical development and the explanation (itself unfortunately almost inexplicable) of the various musical relationships.

By "the law of harmonic progression," Hanslick means the harmonic series of overtones. In Chapter 6, he writes about "the natural harmonics – which ... are the unique and indisputable natural foundation upon which the more complex relationships ... are founded."[7]

All musical elements have mysterious bonds and affinities among themselves, determined by natural laws. These, imperceptibly regulating rhythm, melody, and harmony, require obedience from human music, and they stamp as caprice and ugliness every noncompliant relationship. They reside, though not in a manner open to scientific investigation, instinctively in every cultivated ear, which accordingly perceives the organic, rational coherence of a *group of tones* [*Tongruppe*; this time Cohen does not altogether dodge it: *"group of sounds"*], or its absurdity and unnaturalness, by mere contemplation, ...

The "elements" are the tones. Their "bonds and affinities" [*Verbindungen und Wahlverwandtschaften*] are the various degrees of apparent tension between the various intervals or steps in the major and minor scales, which in turn derive from the "law of harmonic progression":

This ... intrinsic rationality is inherent in the *tonal system* [*Tonsystem*; Cohen: *"music"*] by natural law. In it is grounded the further capacity of *tones* [*dessen*, referring to *Tonsystem*; Cohen: *"its,"* apparently referring to *"music"*] for entering into the positive content of the beautiful.

Composing is a work of mind upon material compatible with mind. This material is immensely abundant and adaptable in the composer's imagination, which builds, not like the architect, out of crude, ponderous stone, but out of the aftereffects of audible *tones* [*Töne*; Cohen: *"sounds"*] already faded away. Being subtler and more ideal than the material of any other art, the *tones* [*Töne*; Cohen: *"sound"*] readily absorb every idea of the composer. Since *tonal connections* [*Tonverbindungen*; Cohen: *"the union of sounds"*], upon the relationships of which musical beauty is based, are achieved not through being linked up mechanically into a series, but by spontaneous activity of the imagination, the spiritual energy and distinctiveness of each composer's imagination make their mark upon the product as character. Accordingly, as the creation of a thinking and feeling mind, a musical composition has in high degree the capability to be itself full of ideality and feeling. This ideal content we demand of every musical artwork. It is to be found only in *the tone-structure itself* [*die Tonbildungen selbst*; Cohen: *"the music itself"*] ...

It is to me inconceivable that Hanslick, when stating the main thesis of his book at a climactic point (the thesis about *tönend bewegte Formen*), would use a *ton-* word (*tönend*, in this case) in a sense other than the predominant sense in which he uses *ton-* words throughout. *Tonkunst* in Hanslick's lifetime was the art not of sounds but of tones; *eine Tondichtung* was a "com-position," tones (not sounds) combined within a relational structure. So:

Der Inhalt der Musik sind tönend bewegte Formen (page 74).

Cohen: The essence of music is sound and motion (page 48).

Payzant: The content of music is tonally moving forms (page 29).

Cohen's word *essence* is pure fantasy. For *essence*, Hanslick regularly uses *das Wesen* or *die Natur; Inhalt* cannot mean anything other than *content* here; it is a very important word in Hanslick's vocabulary, as my sketch regarding *form* and *content* in the first part of this Essay will show. Here we must dismiss Cohen's *essence* as a blunder and concentrate upon *tönend bewegte Formen.*
  Nobody who has tried to translate this expression will fail to sympathize over Cohen's despair as he settled for *"sound and motion."* The problem is not just that there is no exact English equivalent; there is no exact German equivalent either, and there is lack of unanimity among German commentators as to exactly what this very figurative and idiosyncratic expression might mean. Hence it would be unreasonable to expect any English version of the formula to be definitive or even acceptable to a majority of readers. I have no such expectation of my own and hope only to have shown here that my version, with a bit of explanation, is intelligible, which Cohen's would not be with any amount of explanation, and that mine is, moreover, consistent with the prevailing usage in the book with regard to *ton-* words. That *"tonally moving forms"* is a bit peculiar in English merely reflects the idiosyncrasy of the German original.
  If one were to make a major effort to produce the most literal possible English rendering of *tönend bewegte Formen,* the result might be something like

... *"soundingly moving forms."*

In Hanslick's German, *tönend* is an adverb derived from the present participle of the verb *tönen,* which in English can mean "to sound," but which obviously cannot mean "to tone" because, musically, except in now-rare, inappropriate senses, there is no such action and no such verb; if it could, there would have been no problem. But, as I have just said, it is inconceivable that Hanslick at this point would have abandoned the "tone" sense of *ton-* words for the "sound" sense, where throughout the book he uses the former so consistently.

The extremely literal rendering I have given above is, of course, nonsense. Let us now try the other extreme, the freest possible paraphrase:

> The content of music is forms dynamically related, the relationships being those inherent in the diatonic (i.e., tonal) musical system.

I confess I find this a satisfactory paraphrase of the German original so far as the meaning is concerned, provided one understands the special sense of *dynamic* (it is explained in Chapter 2 of Hanslick's book) and of *form* (Chapters 3, 4, 7). But the problem now becomes a literary one for the translator: *Der Inhalt der Musik sind tönend bewegte Formen* is meant to be a ringing declaration, and my paraphrase above, whatever its merits, does not ring.

Hence I am compelled to seek a compromise between meaning and ringing if I am not to do violence to the structure of Chapter 3 and of the whole book. "Tonally moving forms" is my compromise, and this essay is my justification of it.

TRANSLATOR'S NOTES

The following notes are intended only to provide basic documentation for Hanslick's acknowledged sources and some of his unacknowledged ones and to clarify a few of the more obscure points in his text. It is hardly credible that there exists no *commentary* (in the sense of a line-by-line exegesis and critique) on *Vom Musikalisch-Schönen* in any language, but it is true. The present translator hopes to complete such a commentary in the not distant future as a separate and much larger volume.

Translator's Preface

1. Paul Moos, *Moderne Musikästhetik in Deutschland* (Leipzig: Seemann, 1902), p. 79.
2. Paul Moos, *Die Philosophie der Musik von Kant bis Eduard von Hartmann* (Stuttgart: Deutsche Verlags-Anstalt, 1922), p. 213.
3. Eduard Hanslick, *Vom Musikalisch-Schönen*, 13th–15th ed. (Leipzig: Breitkopf & Härtel, 1922).
4. See the preceding Note. Recent editions are numbered in the twenties, but the text is unchanged. The same edition is available in its entirety in Eduard Hanslick, *Vom Musikalisch-Schönen: Aufsätze: Musikkritiken* (Leipzig: Philipp Reclam jun., 1982).
5. Rudolf Schäfke, *Eduard Hanslick und die Musikästhetik* (Leipzig: Breitkopf & Härtel, 1922; reprint ed., Nendeln/Lichtenstein: Kraus, 1976), p. 1.
6. Morris Weitz, ed., *The Beautiful in Music,* by Eduard Hanslick, trans. Gustav Cohen (New York: Liberal Arts Press, 1957), p. vii.
7. *Blätter für Literatur und Kunst: Beilage der Oesterreichische-Kaiserlichen Wiener Zeitung,* No. 34 (21 August 1854), p. 226.
8. Eduard Hanslick, *Aus meinem Leben,* 2 vols. (Berlin, 1894), vol. 1, pp. 237-38.

9. Eduard Hanslick, *Vom Musikalisch-Schönen: ein Beitrag zur Revision der Ästhetik der Tonkunst* (Leipzig, 1854; reprint ed. Darmstadt: Wissenschaftliche Buchgesellschaft, 1981).

10. Hanslick, *Vom Musikalisch-Schönen* (1854), pp. v-vi.

11. Hanslick, *Leben,* vol. 1, pp. 242-3.

12. Immanuel Kant, trans. James W. Ellington, *Grounding for the Metaphysics of Morals* (Indianapolis: Hackett Publishing Company, 1981).

13. "Ed – d," "Zweites Konzert des Cäcilienvereins am 15. Dezember," *Beiblätter zu Ost und West,* No. 203 (19 December 1844), p. 822.

14. J. A. Hanslik signed his two major publications thus. One of them is a history and description of the Prague University Library; the other is mentioned in Note 15 below. Eduard Hanslick, in his first publication to bear his name, signed himself likewise, without the c: Eduard Hanslik, "Ritter Berlioz in Prague." *Ost und West,* No. 9 (22 January 1846), pp. 38-40.

15. J. H. Dambeck, ed. J. A. Hanslik, *Vorlesungen über Aesthetik,* 2 vols. (Prague, 1823).

16. One of the first critiques of *Vom Musikalisch-Schönen,* if not the very first, was written by Robert Zimmermann and published in Eitelberger's *Blätter:* Robert Zimmermann, "Zur Aesthetik der Tonkunst. Vom Musikalisch-Schönen. Von Dr. Eduard Hanslick. . . . " *Blätter für Literatur und Kunst,* No. 47 (20 November 1854), pp. 313-15. Reprinted with minor alterations in Robert Zimmermann, *Zur Aesthetik: Studien und Kritiken* (Vienna, 1870), pp. 239-53. This volume is dedicated to Eduard Hanslick. It erroneously cites No. 11 of *Blätter;* it should be No. 47 as above.

17. Noteworthy among commentators in this regard is Hanslick's friend August Wilhelm Ambros, author of the first book attacking *Vom Musikalisch-Schönen:* A. W. Ambros, *Die Grenzen der Musik und Poesie* (Leipzig, 1855; reprint ed. Hildesheim: Olms, 1976), p. 10; trans. J. H. Cornell, *The Boundaries of Music and Poetry* (New York: 1893), p. 10.

18. F. Printz, *Zur Würdigung des musikästhetischen Formalismus Eduard Hanslicks* (Dissertation, University of Munich, 1918), ch. 1. See also Benedetto Croce, trans. Douglas Ainslie, *Aesthetics as Science of Expression and General Linguistic* (London: Macmillan, 1909), pp. 351-53.

19. Ed. Carl Dahlhaus and Michael Zimmermann, *Musik – zur Sprache gebracht* . . . (Munich: Deutscher Taschenbuch Verlag, and Kassel: Bärenreiter-Verlag Karl Vötterle, 1984), p. 300.

20. C. F. Michaelis, *Ueber den Geist der Tonkunst mit Rücksicht auf Kant's Kritik der Ästhetischen Urtheilskraft.* 2 vols. (Leipzig, 1800; reprint ed. Brussels: *Culture et Civilisation,* 1970).

21. Geoffrey Payzant, "Eduard Hanslick and the 'geistreich' Dr. Alfred Julius

Becher." *The Music Review* 44 (1983): 104-115. In preparation by the same author: a monograph "Eduard Hanslick on 'Ritter Berlioz' in Prague."

22. Chapter 4 and 5 of *Vom Musikalisch-Schönen* appeared *in Blätter für Literatur und Kunst* in three instalments, all under the title "Ueber den subjektiven Eindruck der Musik und seine Stellung in der Aesthetik," the issues of 25 July 1853 (pages 177-78), 1 August 1853 (pages 181-82), and 15 August 1853 (pages 193-95). Chapter 6 was published in the same journal the following year, apparently as an afterthought, with the title as it stands in the book: "Die Tonkunst in ihren Beziehungen zur Natur"; this was in the issue of 13 March 1854 (pages 78-80). The text in these instalments is in no significant way different from the corresponding text in the book.

23. Hanslick, *Leben*, vol. 2, p. 307.

Foreword

1. F. T. Vischer, *Altes und Neues* (Stuttgart, 1882), p. 187.
2. "... auf unmittelbar Evidenz des Gefühls...." The word *Evidenz* is a technical term in German Idealistic philosophy and in Phenomenology. It signifies that in our awareness which is simply given, not subject to proof or disproof; that which thought and knowledge illuminate.
3. Eduard Hanslick, *Musikalische Stationen*, 5th ed. (Berlin, 1885). (Allgemeine Verein für Deutsche Literatur.)
4. Emanuel Geibel, *Gesammelte Werke*, 8 vols. (Stuttgart, 1883), vol. 5, p. 41.

Chapter I

1. I.e., beauty.
2. Robert Schumann, *Gesammelte Schriften über Musik und Musiker*, 4 vols. (Leipzig, 1854), vol. 1, p. 43.
3. Franz Grillparzer, *Sämmtliche Werke*, 10 vols. (Stuttgart, 1872), vol. 9, p. 141.
4. Omitted: "also zwar nur für das Wohlgefallen eines anschauenden Subjekts, aber nicht durch dasselbe." This portion of the text was rewritten for the Second Edition (1858). Apparently these words are vestigial.
5. G. W. F. Hegel, trans. T. M. Knox, *Aesthetics: Lectures on Fine Art*, 2 vols. (Oxford, 1975), vol. 1, p. 32; *Werke*, 19 vols. (Berlin, 1835), vol. 10, p. 43.
6. Hanslick's point here is that the German word *Anschauung* (here trans-

lated "contemplation") derives from *Schau*, the original applications of
which were primarily visual; but that usage had expanded its meaning to
include the other sensory modes and "perception" in no specific sense.
7. I.e., of beauty.
8. Regarding anecdotes about Mozart: Friedrich Rochlitz, *Für Freunde der
Tonkunst*, 3rd ed., 4 vols. (Leipzig, 1868), vol. 1, p. 179n. Regarding
Weber's sonata: review signed "Rochlitz" in *Allgemeine Musikalische
Zeitung*, No. 39 (30 September 1818), p. 686.

Chapter II

1. As we shall see in the sequel, the "concept" of the picture of a flower-girl
is "girlish happiness and innocence." Of the statue, the concept would
perhaps be valor; of the poem, adventurousness.
2. F. T. Vischer, *Aesthetik, oder Wissenschaft des Schönen zum Gebrauche
für Vorlesungen* (Reutlingen & Leipzig, 1864), p. 49. As Hanslick indicates,
the quotation comes from §11; but it is main text, not an *Anmerkung*.
3. Karl Rosenkranz, *Psychologie, oder die Wissenschaft vom subjecktiven
Geist*, 2nd ed. (Königsberg, 1843), p. 100.
4. G. G. Gervinus, *Händel und Shakespeare: zur Ästhetik der Tonkunst*
(Leipzig, 1868), pp. 173-80.
5. Ferdinand Hiller, *Aus dem Tonleben unserer Zeit*, New Series (Leipzig,
1871), pp. 40-42.
6. Heinrich Proch (1809-79) is frequently produced by Hanslick in his early
writings as evidence of the decline in musical taste of his time. Proch's
"Das Alpenhorn," a sentimental lovesong, was one of his more notable
commercial successes, being published in arrangements for various combinations of voices and instruments, and in large numbers. It is but one of
more than two hundred published works of its kind by this composer.
Concerning another of Proch's songs Hanslick wrote, in part: "... 'Frage
nicht' ist aber von einer so abgeläßten, suffisanten Sentimentalität, von
einer so stoppelhaften Geistesdürre,..." (*Ost und West*, No. 57 (9 April
1845), p. 226).
7. This strenuous feat occurs (more than once) in the finale to Bellini's
opera *La Sonnambula*, to Amina's words "Ah mi abbraccia...."
8. Carl von Winterfeld, *Der evangelische Kirchengesang und sein Verhältnis
zur Kunst des Tonsatzes*, 3 vols. (Leipzig, 1847; reprint ed., Hildesheim:
Olms, 1966), pp. 167-69.
9. Eduard Hanslick, *Die Moderne Oper* (Berlin, 1875), pp. 16-17.
10. Johann Mattheson, *Der Vollkommene Kapellmeister* (Hamburg, 1739;
reprint ed. Kassel & Basel: Bärenreiter, 1954), pp. 230-34.
11. Otto Jahn, *W. A. Mozart*, 4 vols. (Leipzig, 1858), vol. 3, pp. 88-92.

12. As cited.
13. *Journal de Politique et de Littérature* (unsigned), October 1777, pp. 168-69.
14. Richard Wagner, *Sämmtliche Schriften und Dichtungen,* 5th ed., 12 vols. (Leipzig: Breitkopf & Härtel, 1911), vol. 3, p. 231.
15. Franz Grillparzer, *Sämmtliche Werke,* 10 vols. (Stuttgart, 1872), vol. 9, pp. 141-46.
16. Ferdinand Hiller, ed., *Briefe von Moritz Hauptmann, Kantor und Musikdirektor an der Thomasschule zu Leipzig, an Ludwig Spohr und Andere* (Leipzig, 1876), p. 106.

Chapter III

1. Because Hanslick's conception of *tonal motion* is central to his argument and because the conception has not been discussed to any great extent in writings about Hanslick in English, I have provided an "Essay: Towards a revised reading of Hanslick" as a supplement to the present translation (see pp. 93-102). The reader is referred to this essay for an introduction to tonal motion and for a guide to the manner in which I have treated Hanslick's vocabulary relating to it.
2. *Satz* in its musical and its logical senses.
3. Franz Grillparzer, *Sämmtliche Werke,* 10 vols. (Stuttgart, 1872), vol. 9, pp. 141-42.
4. A. D. Ulybyschew, trans. A. Shraishuon, *Mozart's Leben,* 3 vols. (Stuttgart, 1847). This is not a quotation, but is apparently a paraphrase of passages in Volume 3, pages 27-33 and 300.
5. Ulybyschew, *Mozart's Leben,* vol. 3, pp. 130-32.
6. Ulybyschew, *Mozart's Leben,* vol. 3, p. 310.
7. The composition is Beethoven's Fantasia in C minor for piano, orchestra, and chorus, op. 80; the painting is "Die Symphonie" by Moritz von Schwind (in the Neue Pinakothek in Munich). The painting is supposed to present visually the very same narrative content as Beethoven presents in his Fantasia. The point of Hanslick's gentle irony ("We are indebted ...") is that this is an impossibility, for the reason that, while painting and poetry derive their content from outside themselves, music does not.
8. "Verfasser der Musikalischen Briefe" (J. C. Lobe), *Fleigende Blätter für Musik* (Leipzig, 1857), p. 89.
9. Otto Jahn, *Gesämmelte Aufsätze über Musik* (Leipzig, 1866), pp. 291-93. The Archduke arrives not in the second section, as in the quotation, but in the third.
10. W. H. Riehl, *Musikalische Charakterköpfe* (Stuttgart & Tübingen, 1853).
11. Eduard Hanslick, *Die Moderne Oper* (Berlin, 1875), pp. vi-viii. Regarding

Hiller on Hasse: perhaps Hanslick refers to a review of the latter by the former in *Wöchentliche Nachrichten und Anmerkungen die Musik betreffend* (14 April 1767), p. 326. Regarding Schubart on Jomelli: C.F.D. Schubart, *Ideen zu einer Ästhetik der Tonkunst* (reprint ed. Leipzig: Reclam, 1977), p. 68.

12. H. C. Oersted, trans. K. L. Kannegiesser, *Neu Beiträge zu dem Geist in der Natur* (Leipzig, 1850), pp. 17-21; trans. L. & J. B. Horner, *The Soul in Nature* (London, 1852), pp. 334-41.

13. Oersted, *Geist*, p. 32; *Soul*, p. 347.

14. In this sentence *sound* translates the German word *Ton*, here used in its general, nonmusical sense.

15. "Musikalische Briefe von einem beschränkten Kopfe." *Allgemeine Zeitung* (Augsburg), No. 217 (5 August 1853), pp. 3465-66. Reprinted in D. F. Strauss, *Kleine Schriften* (Leipzig, 1862), p. 418.

16. Dr. A. J. Becher, "Filharmonische Akademie" (review). *Sonntagsblätter,* No. 13 (26 March 1843), pp. 297, 295. See Geoffrey Payzant, "Eduard Hanslick and the 'Geistreich' Dr. Alfred Julius Becher," *The Music Review* 44 (1983): 104-15.

Chapter IV

1. K. Rosenkranz, *Psychologie, oder die Wissenschaft vom Subjectiven Geist,* 2nd ed. (Königsberg, 1843), pp. 60-61.

2. C.F.D. Schubart, *Ideen zu einer Ästhetik der Tonkunst* (Vienna, 1806), p. 141.

3. C. C. Rolle, *Neue Wahrnehmungen zur Aufnahme und weitern Ausbreitung der Musik* (Berlin, 1784), p. 102.

4. This note appears in the 6th (1881) and subsequent editions of *Vom Musikalisch-Schönen.* H. Dieter's translations into German from A. W. Thayer's (English) manuscripts appeared at irregular intervals beginning in 1866. A. B. Marx, *Ludwig van Beethoven, Leben und Schaffen* (Berlin, 1859); A. W. Thayer, ed. and trans. H. Dieters, *Ludwig van Beethoven's Leben* (Berlin, 1866-).

5. J. N. Forkel, *Ueber die Theorie der Musik, insofern sie Liebhabern und Kennern nothwendig und nützlich ist* (Göttingen, 1777), p. 23.

6. F. T. Vischer, *Aesthetik, oder Wissenschaft des Schönen zum Gebrauchs für Vorlesungen* (Reutlingen & Leipzig, 1864), pp. 122-26.

7. In the 9th (1896) and subsequent editions, *die Reproduktion* is elucidated by the addition of *die Aufführung* ("the performance") thus: " . . . als vielmehr die Reproduktion, die Aufführung, desselben."

8. F. W. Riemer, ed., *Briefwechsel zwischen Goethe und Zelter in den Jahren 1796 bis 1832,* 6 vols. (Berlin, 1834), vol. 3, pp. 331-32.

9. J. W. Albrecht, *Tractatus physicus de effectibus musices in corpus animatum* (Leipzig, 1734), pp. 130-31.

10. H. C. Oersted, trans. K. L. Kannegießer, *Neue Beiträge zu dem Geist in der Natur* (Leipzig, 1850), p. 9; trans. L. & J. B. Horner, *The Soul in Nature* (London, 1852), pp. 329-30.

11. Peter Lichtenthal, *Der musikalische Arzt* (Vienna, 1807), ch. 3. Lichtenthal mentions "stupiditas" on page 143, along with nymphomania, among the disorders amenable to treatment by music.

12. *Encyclopédie ou Dictionnaire raisonné des Sciences, des Arts et des Métiers* (1765), s.v. "Porta"; Giovanbattista Porta, *De i miracoli et maravgliosi effeti dalla natura prodotti* (Venice, 1562), II, xxiv, pp. 88b-90b; trans. Anon., *Natural Magick* (London, 1658; facsimile ed. New York: Basic Books, 1957), pp. 402-5.

13. Daniel Webb, *Observations on the Correspondence between Poetry and Music* (London, 1769), pp. 6-12; trans. J. J. Eschenburg, *Betrachtungen über die Verwandtschaft der Poesie und Musik* (Leipzig, 1771), pp. 4-7. E. A. Nicolai, *Die Verbindung der Musik mit der Arzneygelahrheit* [sic] (Halle, 1745), pp. 1-4 et passim. P. J. Schneider, *System einer medizinischen Musik...*, 2 vols. (Bonn, 1835), vol. 1, pp. 103f.; vol. 2, pp. 176f. Lichtenthal, *Der musikalische Arzt*, p. 57 et passim. J. J. Engel, *Über die musikalische Malerei* (Berlin, 1780), pp. 18-23; *Schriften*, 12 vols. (Berlin, 1802), vol. 4, pp. 297-342. J. G. Sulzer, *Allgemeine Theorie der schönen Künste* (Leipzig, 1771-74), s.v. "Musik."

14. Robert Boyle, "Some considerations touching the Usefulness of Experimental Natural Philosophy," *The Works of the Honourable Robert Boyle,* 6 vols. (London, 1772), vol. 2, p. 176.

15. J. J. Kausch, *Psychologische Abhandlung über den Einfluß der Töne und ins besonders der Musik auf die Seele* (etc.) (Breslau, 1782).

16. Kausch (*Psychologische Abhandlung,* pp. 151-52) mentions "der große Engländer Whytt," who turns out to be Robert Whyte of Edinburgh, who wrote *Observations on the Nature, Causes, and Cure of those Disorders which have been commonly called Nervous, Hypochondriac, or Hysteric* (etc.) (Edinburgh, 1765). Whyte is misrepresented by both Kausch and Hanslick. In his first chapter ("Of the structure, use, and sympathy of the nerves") Whyte says that *none* of the nerves are connected to any others as are, for example, the blood vessels. The nerves interact only sympathetically (referred pain would be an example) through the mediation of what he calls the *sensorium commune,* which Whyte says belongs to the divine mysteries. A German translation of Whyte's *Observations* appeared in Leipzig in 1771 as *Robert Whytt's Sämmtlich zur praktischen Arzneykunst gehörige Schriften.*

17. A person by the name of Goldberger is mentioned as the inventor of two

electrotherapeutic devices in R.-A. Lewandowski, *Elektrodiagnostik und Elektrotherapie...* (Vienna and Leipzig, 1887), pp. 206, 351. Lewandowski says that Goldberger and others had marketed their electromagnetic chains in charlatanish fashion.

18. Hermann von Helmholtz, *Die Lehre von den Tonempfindungen* (Brunswick, 1863).

19. C. Harless, "Hören" in R. Wagner, *Handwörterbuch der Physiologie mit Rücksicht auf physiologische Pathologie,* 4 vols. (Brunswick, 1853), vol. 4, p. 423; C. G. Carus, *System der Physiologie,* 3 vols. (Dresden & Leipzig, 1840), vol. 3, pp. 113-17.

20. J. E. Purkinje (1787-1869), professor of pathology and physiology at Prague and Breslau, author of a famous book about the central nervous system.

21. Helmholtz, *Tonempfindungen,* 3rd ed. (Brunswick, 1870), p. 319. (Hanslick cites the wrong edition.)

22. R. H. Lotze, *Medicinische Psychologie* (Leipzig, 1852), pp. 273, 264.

23. E. Du Bois-Reymond, *Über die Grenzen des Naturerkennens* (Leipzig, 1872), pp. 25, 33 et passim.

24. Johann Mattheson, *Der vollkommene Kapellmeister* (Hamburg, 1739; reprint ed. Kassel & Basel: Bärenveiter, 1954), p. 18.

25. J. D. Heinichen, *Der General-Baß in der Composition* (etc.) (Dresden, 1728), pp. 32-88 approx. Hanslick's *"acht Bogen Notenbeispiele"* is usually translated "eight pages of music examples," but *Bogen* means "sheet of paper," hence in this case eight sheets folded in quarto, making thirty-two leaves or sixty-four pages of text, which is roughly the length of the passage in question. Hanslick's remark concerning Heinichen (often, as here, spelled *Heinchen*) is taken almost verbatim from Mattheson, *Kapellmeister,* pp. 16-17.

26. F.F.S.A. von Boecklin von Boecklins-Au, *Fragmente zur höhern Musik, und für ästhetische Tonliebhaber* (Freiburg & Constance, 1811), p. 34. Hanslick here pokes fun at the author, who on his title page describes himself as "geheim Rathe von Böcklin, der Philosophie Doktor, der Akademie der Arkadier zu Rom, wie auch verschiedener gelehrten Gesellschaften, Mitgliede u."

27. Reading "einbringt" for "eingeht."

Chapter V

1. I.e., the specifically musically beautiful.
2. In Hanslick's vocabulary an "enthusiast" is anyone who listens to music primarily for its emotional or physical rather than for its intellectual effects.

3. One of Hanslick's more tangled webs. There is a book by A. Burgh with the title *Anecdotes of Music, Historical and Biographical* (etc.) (London, 1814), but the Palma anecdote is not in it. Yet it is in A. Burgh, trans. C. F. Michaelis, *Anekdoten und Bemerkungen, Musik betreffend* (Leipzig, 1820), p. 75. This volume is in fact not a translation of Burgh's book but a collection of anecdotes (including some from Burgh) about one-third the length of Burgh. It mentions "Martinelli" as the source of the Palma anecdote but gives no bibliographical information. The "translator" Michaelis may have taken it from *Wöchentliche Nachrichten und Anmerkungen die Musik betreffend* (20 January 1767), p. 233; his version is different only in the most insignificant details. *Wöchentliche Nachrichten* on page 232 attributes the anecdote to Martinelli; the previous issue (13 January 1767) announces the beginning of a new series of such anecdotes under the general title "Ueber die Musik," these having been recently published in *Dictionnaire d'Anecdotes*. There is a work with that title, published at Paris in 1766; Palma is in the second volume on page 498. Page 494 attributes the Palma anecdote to "M. Martinelli, auteur de quelques lettres critiques sur la musique Italienne...." These turn out to be *Lettere familiari e critiche* by V. Martinelli (London, 1758); our story is on page 367. I followed the trail no further.

4. Plato, *Republic* III.

5. Letter of Beethoven to Bettina von Arnim dated August 1812: "... Rührung paßt nur für Frauenzimmer (Verzeih' mir's), dem Mann muß Musikfeuer aus dem Geist schlagen." In A. Schindler, ed. from 3rd edition (1860) by F. Volbach, *Ludwig van Beethoven* (Münster: Aschendorff, 1927), p. 351. Note that Beethoven says *must*, not *should*.

6. F. Hand, *Aesthetik der Tonkunst,* 2 vols. (Leipzig, 1857), vol. 1, pp. 45-46; trans. W. E. Lawson, *Aesthetics of Musical Art* (London, 1880), p. 59. For elephants: *Allgemeine Musikalische Zeitung,* No. 19 (6 February 1799), pp. 298-304. For spiders: ibid., No. 20 (13 February 1799), p. 318; No. 37 (11 June 1800), pp. 653-56.

7. For sources of this anecdote, see O. Strunk, *Source Readings in Music History* (New York & London: W. W. Norton & Co., 1950), pp. 282, 319. It can be found in many of Hanslick's sources cited elsewhere in these Notes, including Forkel, Kausch, and Rousseau.

8. Albert Krantz, *Rerum Germanicarum historici clariss. Regnorum Aquilonarium, Daniae, Sueciae, Noruagiae, Chronica* (Frankfurt, 1583), pp. 99-100. (Hanslick's citation of Book V, Chapter 3 is correct.)

9. Hanslick's sources for this extraordinary account of the music of the ancient Greeks perhaps include Forkel, Kiesewetter, and Marpurg. Perhaps it is here just to set us up for the shaggy-dog ending.

10. The German *genießen,* of which *Genuß* (enjoyment, pleasure, etc.) is a

derivation, is etymologically linked to the verb *nutzen* (to make use of, turn to account, etc.). Hanslick's remark calls attention to the active and transitive nature of musical contemplation.

11. F. W. J. Schelling, *Über das Verhältniß der bildenden Künste zu der Natur* (Vienna, 1825), p. 27; *Werke* (Munich, 1859), 3. Ergänzungsband, p. 407.

12. Wilhelm Heinse, ed. C. Schüddekopf, *Sämmtliche Werke*, 10 vols. (Leipzig: Insel-Verlag, 1913), vol. 5, pp. 33-34.

13. Hanslick perhaps has in mind Goethe's letter to Bettina dated 3 August 1808: "Die besten Stunden benütze ich dazu, um näher mit ihnen vertraut zu werden, und ermuthige mich, die elektrischen Schläge deiner Begeistrungen auszuhalten. . . . Du hast zwar flammende Fackeln und Feuerbecken ausgestellt in der Finsterniß, aber bis jetzt blenden sie mehr als sie erleuchten, indessen erwarte ich doch von der ganzen Illumination einen herrliche Totaleffekt, so bleibe nur dabei und sprühe nach allen Seiten hin." *Goethe's Briefwechsel mit einem Kinde*, 3rd ed. (Berlin, 1849), first part, pp. 285-86. Bettina published privately her own English translation in two volumes as *Goethe's Correspondence with a Child: for his Monument* (no title page, no date). She translates the foregoing as follows: "My best hours I use in becoming more nearly acquainted with them [i.e., with Bettina's enthusiastic remarks about music in her letters to Goethe], and I encourage myself to endure the electric shocks of your inspiration. . . . It is true, you have placed amidst the darkness flaming torches and fire-basons; but at present they dazzle more than they illuminate; – yet at the same time I expect from the entire illumination a splendid 'total effect,' therefore continue sparking on all sides." (Vol. 1, pp. 296-98.)

14. Aristophanes, *Wasps* 1244. Aristophanes here is not talking about the attributes of cultivated persons but is making an ironic remark about a particular man neither cultivated nor musical nor wise. Hanslick's point eludes me.

15. K. F. Graf von Reinhard [sic], letter to Goethe dated 14 October 1807. In *Goethe und Reinhard Briefwechsel in den Jahren 1807-1832* (Wiesbaden: Insel-Verlag, 1957), p. 45.

Chapter VI

1. H. G. Nägeli, *Vorlesungen über Musik* (Stuttgart & Tübingen, 1826), p. 200.

2. Ferdinand Hand, *Aesthetik der Tonkunst*, 2 vols. (Leipzig, 1857), vol. 1, pp. 48-50; trans. W. E. Lawson, *Aesthetics of Musical Art* (London, 1880), pp. 62-65.

3. M. Hauptmann, *Die Natur der Harmonik und der Metrik* (Leipzig, 1853), p. 7.

4. Jacob Grimm, *Über den Ursprung der Sprache* (Berlin, 1852), p. 54.
5. J. Kinkel, *Acht Briefe an eine Freundin über Clavier-Unterricht* (Stuttgart & Tübingen, 1852), p. 76.
6. Hand, *Tonkunst,* vol. 1, ch. 1, "Von der Musik der Natur überhaupt." Hand consistently maintains that, in the strict sense of the word *music,* there is no music in nature. He concedes that "it is generally recognized that, in the voice of the bird, which amongst animals alone sings, we first meet with that which may be regarded as music [*was als Musik betrachtet werden könnte*]" (*Musical Art,* p. 51; *Tonkunst,* vol. 1, p. 39). This is as close as Hand comes to *gewissermaßen.* But see Note 7 next.
7. E. Krüger, *Beiträge für Leben und Wissenschaft der Tonkunst* (Leipzig, 1847), pp. 139-52 et passim. The *gewissermaßen* of the preceding note may have come from Krüger's *Beitrage, p.* 141, where architecture "in a manner of speaking" imitates nature, and this view is extended to music on the following page. But Krüger denies that there can be a connection between bird song and human music, because birds do not sing in commensurable tones (p. 142).
8. Precisely the opposite is argued by Hand: "Where the power of self-energy does not make itself known, nor that which is inward and spiritual express itself, tones are but the result of external circumstances, or of a corporeal, but not free activity. Just as the flute clock, by means of a mechanism which in itself is dead, performs even works of art, the action which mechanically repeats them being but the product of human ingenuity, so the song of birds lacks the expression of a free inner life, for they sing mostly at a time when they are influenced by sexual instinct" (*Musical Art,* pp. 51-52).
9. A thesis or maxim about "the imitation of nature in art" will prove difficult to locate in Aristotle's works, at least in the senses of *art, nature,* and even *imitation* used by Hanslick. Insofar as Aristotle may be said to have a theory of what we call the "fine arts," a concept of *imitation* is central to that theory, although Aristotle does not tell us precisely what he means by *imitation.*
10. Letter of J. P. F. Richter to Paul Thieriot dated 17 January 1801. In Ernst Förster, ed., *Denkwürdigkeiten aus dem Leben von Jean Paul Friedrich Richter,* 4 vols. (Munich, 1863), vol. 1, p. 431.
11. I have found no such remark by Otto Jahn. However, it may be a paraphrase of passages from Jahn's delightful essay "Beethoven im Malkasten" in *Allgemeine Musikalische Zeitung,* No. 17 (22 April 1863), pp. 293-99; *Gesammelte Aufsätze über Musik* (Leipzig, 1866), pp. 260-70. (This footnote first appeared in the sixth (1881) edition of *Vom Musikalisch-Schönen.*)

Chapter VII

1. As cited. This volume is Part Two of Zimmermann's two-volume *Aesthetik*, identified on its title page as the "systematic" part. Part One is the "historical-critical" part: *Geschichte der Aesthetik als Philosophischer Wissenschaft* (Vienna, 1858).
2. J. J. Rousseau, *Dictionnaire de Musique* (Paris, 1768), s.v. "Musique" et passim. Immanuel Kant, *Kritik der Urteilskraft* in *Gesammelte Schriften*, 22 vols. (Berlin: Prussian Academy, 1908), vol. 5; trans. J. H. Bernard, *Critique of Judgment* (New York: Hafner, 1951), §16, §51, §53-54. G. W. F. Hegel, *Vorlesungen über die Ästhetik*, in *Werke*, 19 vols. (Berlin, 1842-43), vol. 10; trans. T. M. Knox, *Aesthetics: Lectures on Fine Art*, 2 vols. (Oxford, 1975), vol. 2, sect. 3, ch. 2 "Music." J. F. Herbart, *Kurze Enzyklopädie der Philosophie*, in *Werke*, 19 vols. (Langensalza, 1897), vol. 9, ch. 9 "Von der schönen Kunst." A. Kahlert, *System der Aesthetik* (Leipzig, 1846).
3. Hermann Lotze, *Geschichte der Aesthetik in Deutschland* (Munich, 1868), pp. 461-504. Hermann von Helmholtz, *Die Lehre von den Tonempfindungen* (Brunswick, 1863).
4. A shotgun metaphor. The verb I have translated as *let off* is *ausgelassen* in the first four editions of *Vom Musikalische-Schönen*, *losgelassen* in the fifth (1876) and subsequent editions. The two barrels of the gun are the two parts of the vociferation: 1. Music exalts and inspires, etc. 2. Music cannot be contentless. Hanslick's point is that the second does not follow from the first.
5. Kahlert, *Aesthetik*, p. 380.
6. E. Krüger, *Beiträge für Leben und Wissenschaft der Tonkunst* (Leipzig, 1847), pp. 131-32, 138.
7. G. E. Lessing, *Laokoön*, in *Werke*, 8 vols. (Munich: Hanser, 1974), vol. 6.
8. In the first eight editions: "... da muß jeder Musiker, ohne von der weiteren Durchführung noch eine Note zu wissen, erkennen vor welchem Palast er steht." In the ninth (1896) and subsequent editions *muß* is softened to *wird* and *erkennen* to *ahnen*. The later version could be translated "... then every musician, without hearing another note of the piece, will have some idea of which palace he stands before."
9. Hanslick introduces the words *geistige Gehalt* in Chapter 3, where I translated them *ideal content* rather than *ideal substance*, for the reason that the distinction between *Inhalt* and *Gehalt* is not there developed. But here in the concluding chapter the distinction becomes crucial. *Inhalt* is content in the sense that the literary and visual arts have content but music has not. *Gehalt* is content in a sense peculiar to musical themes. It is the source of their "efficacy and fecundity" [*Kraft und Fruchbarkeit*]. *Gehalt* reveals the spiritual depth and individuality of the composer as

creative spirit, and marks the essential characteristic of each musical work, i.e., that which distinguishes it from every other work of similar "abstract feeling content." *Inhalt* is *transcendent; Gehalt* is *immanent.*

10. Hanslick's posturing with Hegelian catchwords makes of these paragraphs a most unsatisfactory ending to his book. Evidently he thinks that, by *subjectivity,* Hegel means only *feeling* or *affect.* And with *renunciation* and *individuality* in their Hegelian applications, he seems wholly unacquainted.

Essay: Towards a Revised Reading of Hanslick

1. Eduard Hanslick, trans. Gustav Cohen, *The Beautiful in Music: a Contribution to the Revisal of Musical Aesthetics* (London and New York: Novello, 1891). In this essay, I cite the reprint edition, ed. Morris Weitz (New York: Liberal Arts Press, 1957).

2. Payzant, p. xxii. (In this essay, I shall refer to the present translation as "Payzant" for purposes of citation.)

3. Payzant, p. xxii.

4. Payzant, p. xxiii.

5. Payzant, p. 71. Eduard Hanslick, *Vom Musikalisch-Schönen: ein Beitrag zur Revision der Ästhetik der Tonkunst,* 8th ed. rev. (Leipzig: Johann Ambrosius Barth, 1891), p. 188.

6. Geoffrey Payzant, "Hanslick, Sams, Gay, and 'tönend bewegte Formen'," *Journal of Aesthetics and Art Criticism* 40 (1981): 41-48.

7. Payzant, p. 71.

INDEX OF PERSONS

INDEX OF SUBJECTS